Child Maintenance

How to Respond to Misbehavior
Without Using
Force, Rewards, or Punishments

by

Michael Pastore

Zorba Press
Ithaca, New York, USA
https://ZorbaPress.com

Child Maintenance : How to Respond to Misbehavior
Without Using Force, Rewards, or Punishments.

ISBN: 9780927379434

For more information about this book
and other books published by Zorba Press
contact us
email: books@zorbapress.com

Release date: 2021-March-28

Printed and bound in the United States of America.
Printings: cm-cov-014, cm-inp-014
0102030405060708091011121314151617181920

Visit our website about Child Maintenance
https://ChildMaintenance.page

Published by Zorba Press
https://ZorbaPress.com

Contents

Part B: The Theory of Child Maintenance

Four Gems of Wise Advice

Be calm, stoical, impassive.
Do not show anger.
Smile at misfortune.
If you sprain your ankle, laugh.

— Tiger Tinaka's advice to secret agent 007, James Bond,
in the novel by Ian Fleming: *You Only Live Twice*

Power is like holding an egg in the palm of your hand.
If you hold too tight you crush the egg,
if you hold too loosely you drop the egg and it breaks.

— African Proverb

The more complex the mind
the greater the need
for the simplicity of play.

— Captain James T. Kirk, *Star Trek: Shore Leave*

Today, I know from experience
that punishment is unnecessary.
I never punish a child,
never have any temptation to punish a child.

— A. S. Neill, *Summerhill*

Part A

The Practice of Child Maintenance

Chapter 1

Siddhartha and His Wild Son

Siddhartha, the hero of the novel by Hermann Hesse, is a seeker of wisdom, enlightenment, and inner peace. He had trained his mind so that he could accomplish any goal. When he was hungry he found food; when he felt lonely he found love; when he was poor he worked smartly to run a business and become rich. Yet there was one goal Siddhartha could not accomplish — he could not manage his 11-year-old son.

By meditation and reflection, Siddhartha had taught himself three essential things. Siddhartha explains this to his future beloved, the intelligent Kamala:

"Anyone can perform magic, anyone can reach his goals if he can can learn how to think, how to wait, and how to fast."

Think. Wait. Fast.

These are the skill sets necessary for a man on a journey to find and to realize his true self. Had Siddhartha remained alone, these skills — along with the art of Listening — would have been enough. Fortunately, in novels, as in life, things happen unexpectedly. At the age of 40, Siddhartha meets his son for the first time, and he loves his son with an unselfish and an overwhelming love. And now, as a single parent, Siddhartha takes on the enormous responsibility of caring for his only child.

Siddhartha had given up his riches and his fine clothes, to live in a hut beside the river, with his aged friend, the ferryman Vasudeva. The son had no taste for living in such an isolated place, the son had no interest in attaining spiritual wisdom. The son wanted to continue his life of luxury and ease, the life he had enjoyed in a bustling city with his mother, the beautiful Kamala.

Two times in his life, Siddhartha had rejected this consuming lifestyle, and now he could never go back. It was natural to expect the boy to feel miserable, and eventually to rebel.

"Siddhartha had called himself rich and happy when the boy first came to see him.

Meanwhile, as time passed, the boy remained withdrawn and sad. He revealed a selfish and defiant heart, he did not want to do even the smallest bit of work, he showed his father and his father's friend Vasudeva no respect, he stole fruit from Vasudeva's orchard. Gradually, Siddhartha began to understand that his son was not happy and would not bring peace to him, but only worry and suffering."

Quickly, things go from bad to worse to impossible. Siddhartha's friend, the wise Vasudeva, tries to make Siddhartha understand what must be done.

"Tell me, my dear: you are not raising your son? You are not forcing him to do things? You are not hitting him? You are not punishing him?"

"No, Vasudeva, I won't do any of that."

"I knew it. You don't force him, you don't hit him, you don't order him to do things because you know that soft is stronger than hard, water is stronger than rock, love is stronger than violence. Very good, I praise you."

One morning, the boy steals the rowboat, takes it across the river, and then runs back to the city where he was born. As an unsubtle message to his father, the boy breaks the oar. Sadly, heartbreakingly, Siddhartha realizes that he should not follow his son. The boy will be safer and happier living with the relatives of Siddhartha's deceased wife.

Siddhartha's three skills — to think, to wait, and to fast — are perfect for the life of solitude and the quest for self-realization. These skills are not good enough for the tasks of child maintenance. The three skills needed for taking care of children — and for solving almost all problems in life — are these:

1. Prevent
2. Respond
3. Nourish

Child Maintenance (this book you are holding in your hands, or reading on a screen) discusses how to Prevent and Nourish, and focuses mainly on the question:

"How should I Respond when children misbehave?"

Child maintenance is the art, and the loving work, of keeping a child in optimum physical and psychological health. The goal of child maintenance is to nourish happy children, kids who are able to play, to love, to learn, to create, to appreciate Nature, and to think soundly.

Let us now leave Siddhartha — smiling and listening deeply to the river — and begin our journey on the path of harmonious relationships with the children in our care.

Everyone can live and work happily with children, if we can learn three types of things: how to prevent, how to respond, and how to nourish.

♥

Chapter 2

12 Essential Terms in Child Maintenance

Before we classify the types of problematic behaviors (in Chapter 3) it will be useful to examine and understand 12 essential terms which will appear throughout the remainder of this book.

These are:

◆ Child maintenance
◆ Child maintenance, goals of
◆ Child-maintenance worker (CMW)
◆ Do-it-or-else! Method
◆ "Freedom, not License"
◆ Misbehavior
◆ Montagu's Maxim
◆ Opportunity-Problem (O-P)
◆ Pastore Principle
◆ Problematic behavior
◆ Resilience
◆ Zerp Factor, and Zerp's Law

Child maintenance is the art, and the joyful work, of keeping a child in optimum physical and psychological health: giving the child the physical and emotional nourishment that s/he needs so that s/he will be able to love, to learn, to play, to appreciate nature, to create, and to think soundly.

Child maintenance, essential goals of. The essence of Child Maintenance is a three-part strategy for working with all types of children. The adult attempts to:
1) Prevent misbehavior: by listening, by respecting children (by not yelling, not threatening, etc.), and by teaching children the meaning of 'Freedom, not license'.
2) Respond whenever children misbehave, respond with words and actions that are calm, creative, and kind.
3) Nourish children by giving children what they need to enjoy a safe and happy childhood.

Child-maintenance worker (abbreviated CMW) is anyone who works with kids: a parent, a teacher, a counselor, a camp counselor or camp staff member, a childcare worker, a grandparent, a nanny, and more.

Do-it-or-else! Method of child control is also called, the Way of Force. This barbaric and uncreative method may be summarized in one cold sentence: "Tell the child what to do; if he disobeys you, then threaten and punish him." The use of force — punishment, threats, intimidation, anger — is a foolish, boorish, and lose-lose attempt to control a child's behavior.

Freedom, not license. This is a basic principle of human relations, formulated by A.S. Neill and practiced in his school named Summerhill. Concisely stated: "Children should be given freedom to do what they like, but no one is allowed to hurt others, or to restrict another person's freedom." This abuse of freedom is called license. Erich Fromm, in his foreword to A.S. Neill's book *Summerhill*, explains it this way: "Freedom does not mean license. This very important principle, emphasized by Neill, is that respect for the individual must be mutual. A teacher does not use force against a child, nor has a child the right to use force against a teacher. A child may not intrude upon an adult just because he is a child, nor may a child use pressure in the many ways in which a child can."

Misbehavior is action that violates the principle of 'Freedom, not License', i.e., any action that hurts another person or living thing, or restricts the freedom of another person. What causes children's misbehavior? Erich Fromm writes: "Destructiveness is the outcome of unlived lives." A. S. Neill writes: "The difficult child is the child who is unhappy. He is at war with himself; and thus he is at war with the whole world." Of course, the caring grownup, knowing that unhappiness causes misbehavior, treats the root of the misbehavior by practicing the three essentials goals of child maintenance.

Montagu's Maxim is a quote by Ashley Montagu:
"A human being should always respond, but never react."

Opportunity-Problem (O-P) is any behavior problem or situation with an outcome that depends on the response of the grownup. React with force and punishment, and you worsen the behavior and antagonize the child. Respond with sincerity and kindness, and you help to heal the root of the misbehavior and deepen your rapport with the child. The ten Opportunity-Problems in this book are taken from the book *101 Problems in Child Maintenance*.

Problematic Behavior (P-B) is a better term — more accurate and more comprehensive — for "misbehavior", because misbehavior implies that the problem is the fault of the child. Frequently, children have many problems that they did not cause. Problematic Behavior is any situation involving a child or children that requires care and attention from the grownups who care for them.

Resilience. What is resilience? Resilience is the inner strength — of body, heart, or mind — to bounce back and stand up again, after something hurts you and knocks you down. Whatever the problem is — a sudden sickness, a drastic change, or a storm of bad luck — a resilient person faces the challenges with honesty and courage. [Definition by MP]. Great CMWs always teach children the art of resilience.

In poetry, a beautiful example of resilience is the inspiring poem *Still I Rise*, by Maya Angelou (1928–2014). In novels, resilience is illustrated in the book by Alexandre Dumas (père), *The Count of Monte Cristo*.

We Technique is a method for responding to misbehavior that lets the child or the children help the grownup to solve the problem. Do this by asking the child or children: "We have a problem — what can we do to solve it?"

Zerp Factor and **Zerp's Law** are named from the character named Zerp, in the novel *Zen In The Art Of Child Maintenance*.

The **Zerp factor** is the tendency of aggressive children — who desperately need caring human contact and affection — to not get that affection because their aggressive behavior drives children and adults away. The antidote to the Zerp Factor is to heal child with child maintenance, the strategy to Prevent, to Respond, and to Nourish.

Zerp's Law says: "When children misbehave they need more sincerity and kindness, not less."

♥

The greatest problem for any thinker
is stating the problem in a way
that will allow a solution.

— Bertrand Russell

Chapter 3

Understanding the 10 Types of Problematic Behavior

When we see adults shouting at kids, punishing kids, and/or doing nothing when something needs to be done — we see adults who are thoroughly unprepared. How can we prepare to work with modern kids?

There are 3 steps:
1) Learn about the various types of problematic behavior.
2) See how these behaviors can be organized into ten useful types.
3) Learn nonaggressive techniques for responding.

Identifying the problem — making an accurate diagnosis — is the first step to applying treatments that can help, cure, and heal.

Children's Problematic Behavior (PB) may be classified into ten types. These types frequently overlap, and often the PB will fall into more than one category.

10 Types of Problematic Behavior

A. Vitality Problems

B. Adultogenic Problems

C. Personal Problems

D. Respect Problems

E. Safety and Health Problems

F. Motivation Problems

G. Money, Property, and Things Problems

H. Interpersonal Problems

I. Passiveness-Listlessness Problems

J. Aggression Problems

Understanding the 10 Types of Problematic Behavior

A. Vitality Problems

Kids have more vitality and energy than most adults. There are many situations which might appear to be problematic behavior, but in reality they are not PB. Often, when children behave naturally and express their unique vitality, an authoritarian adult will intervene and stop a behavior that is natural and does not need to be corrected.

B. Adultogenic Problems

Have you ever walked into a dentist's office to get your teeth cleaned, and when you come out you notice that the dental surgeon has extracted your perfectly healthy left molar? Let's hope not. This is called an iatrogenic problem: a problem caused by the doctor. Similarly, I have coined the term Adultogenic Problems. These are children's behavior problems which are caused by adults: by unnecessary restrictions, by rules not in the best interests of the child, by unfair conditions, or by harsh punishments.

C. Personal Problems
In this group the child is usually fighting against himself. Problems here include fears, sadness, and love-or-sex-relationship problems.

D. Respect Problems
Respect means respect for the freedom and rights of other persons, and respect for nonhuman living beings. This type of problem encompasses all the situations when the child interferes with the freedom of other persons — children or adults — or harms nonhuman living beings.

E. Safety and Health Problems
This category includes the large group of situations where the child's action — or actions he neglects — endanger the safety or health of himself or others.

F. Motivation Problems
These problems arise when the child has not done something that needs to be done.

G. Money, Property, and Things Problems
This group comprises almost all problems involving conflicts (including theft and damage) about money, property, and things.

H. Interpersonal Problems
Place in this group most of the problems — there are so many! — between one child and another child, or one child and an adult, or one child and his group of peers.

I. Passiveness-Listlessness Problems
Children who've lost interest in and enthusiasm for the activities that genuinely nourish their minds, bodies, and hearts — such as couch-potato-kids addicted to video games and TV — fall into this lethargic group.

J. Aggression Problems
This category contains some of the most difficult situations that adults must face: when the child harms himself or another child, or threatens this kind of harm.

In the previous chapter, Chapter 2, we reviewed twelve important terms, including what we call Problematic Behavior: situations which require helping intervention from adults.

In this chapter, Chapter 3, we divided this universe of Problematic Behavior into ten varieties of problems.

In the next chapter, Chapter 4, we will explore alternatives to punishment, and offer more than ten techniques for teaching and helping our kids.

♥

Chapter 4

The 10 New Techniques for Responding To Problematic Behavior

Each child, like every moment in our lives, is special and unique. We will never be able to live wisely and happily if we pretend otherwise, if we attempt to manage our children by formulas or recipes. Life is more complex than that. Ideally, we should teach ourselves how to see as children and artists see: to see each moment and each object as fresh, spontaneous, and new. And we should learn how to respond to each new situation with a personal response, a response we invent after intensely concentrating our entire creative and loving energies.

What I am talking about is similar to improvisation. But there is all the difference in the world between what casually tumbles off the top of your head, and what naturally springs from the bottom of your heart. It takes many years of practice before our intuitions and expertise can rise to the level where we can soundly improvise.

Until then, we can learn the tools of our craft the same way that writers, artists, and musical composers learn: by studying and practicing from good examples. This chapter will introduce you to ten techniques that have one thing in common: they work. The ultimate goal is to master these, to have each one of them ready in your mind to be applied when needed, then to create your own nonaggressive responses to help to heal children's problematic behavior.

How To Think About
Applying These Methods In Practice

How does a skilled parent or child-maintenance worker think — what goes on inside her mind — when she encounters children behaving problematically? ... Let's first examine the way she does NOT think. She knows from experience that punishment fails completely. She knows that if she punishes the child for misbehavior, he will not learn to become a self-reliant child, capable of thinking for himself, and behaving well when no one is around to watch.

But she also knows that she cannot sit back and watch (or go away and fail to watch): her first responsibility is to protect the child and the children from harming themselves or others. Let's enter the mind of the skilled parent or child-maintenance worker who reflects about how to respond to the child's problematic behavior (PB).

Before the PB, our skilled parent or child-maintenance worker has established a sincere rapport with each child she is caring for. This rapport is essential: without the rapport, many problems are impossible to solve. With the rapport, many so-called 'difficult' problems become simple.

When the problematic behavior occurs, she makes certain that she is calm and relaxed — she knows that throughout history, children have misbehaved and she is not shocked when it happens again.

Observing the situation, she very quickly summarizes the problem, then in her mind places the problem into one of the ten types explained in Chapter 3.

If the problematic behavior endangers the child, or endangers other children, then the parent or child-maintenance worker will immediately stop this behavior. If there is no immediate danger involved, then the parent or child-maintenance worker will take a little time to respond.

Now the parent or child-maintenance worker will respond (not react!) by thinking of a number of alternative methods she could use to meet the situation. Whenever appropriate, she will let the child or other children help her to solve the problem. From her mental menu of options she will select the one she believes will work the best in this case. She views this as an experiment: if it turns out to be not working, then she will change her course.

When she applies this method or technique, she speaks to the child in a calm and caring tone of voice. (If she cannot meet the situation calmly, she will withdraw and find an adult who can.) After her initial response, she makes a note to follow up by spending more time with this child. Her ultimate goal is to try to discover the underlying cause of the problematic behavior, and to treat the underlying cause.

Now we will summarize the general method that our skilled parent or child-maintenance worker practices whenever she encounters PB with kids.

The C.A.R.I.N.G.
6-Step Strategy For Thinking About then Responding
To Problematic Behavior

Calm Yourself. Always be calm.

The parent or child-maintenance worker remains calm whenever children engage in problematic behavior. Always, the parent or child-maintenance worker speaks to the child — and applies the response techniques — in a calm and caring voice. If the child is upset, she first calms the child.

Analyze the Problem.

When the problematic behavior (PB) occurs, the parent or child-maintenance worker quickly classifies the type of PB. The most important facet of this analysis is answering the question: Is this behavior harming the child, another person, or another living being?

If the answer to this question is 'Yes,' then this type of behavior is called 'Endangering Behavior.' (See Chapter 3 for a list of ten problem types, A to J.)

Respond Immediately to Stop the Endangering Behavior.

If the PB endangers the child or other children, then it must be immediately stopped. If there is no danger to the children, then continue to the next step — step 4, below.

I **magine** Three Alternative Response Options.
The parent or child-maintenance worker, in her mind, creates and examines at least three alternative ways to respond. These three alternatives must be without force, threats, violence, punishments, and rewards.

The **Quick Chart** in Chapter 15 can be used as a guide to selecting the best responses based on the type of Problematic Behavior.

N **ow** Choose The Best Option.
After evaluating the 3 options, the parent or CMW selects and applies the response which appears to be the best one.

G **ive** Emotional Support Before and After Problematic Behavior.
Before the PB, the parent or child-maintenance worker has established a sincere, caring rapport with each child. An important facet of this rapport is the parent or child-maintenance worker's resolve never to use rewards, and never to use the way of force: threats, anger, intimidation, or punishments.

After the PB — and after the parent or child-maintenance worker's calm, caring, creative response — the parent or child-maintenance worker follows up on the situation by listening and talking, and by nourishing the child with one or more of his basic needs.

An Overview of the Ten Techniques

Here are the ten techniques — 10 options that a skilled parent or child-maintenance worker will have at hand, ready to apply in the right situation at the right time.

1. Acceptance
2. Change the Circumstances
3. Listening and Talking
4. Teach the basic principle of 'Freedom, not License.'
5. Creative Role-Playing (CRP)
6. Motivation Techniques
7. Pedocracy: The Government by Children
8. Interpersonal Techniques
9. Give the Child a 'Time-In'
10. Intervene Now! then L. E. N. D.

    (Listen, Explain, Nourish, Design)

A Summary of the Ten Techniques

1. Acceptance.

At times, when the child's behavior might appear to be problematic but actually is not, then the best thing to do is to accept it and not to interfere.

2. Change the Circumstances.

Many (too many) problematic behaviors are caused by adults who are too strict, rules which are unfair, and environments which are too restrictive.

Often in these situations, the right response is to change the circumstances to undo our mistakes, and to accommodate the child's needs.

3. Listening and Talking.

A thousand years of shouting is not worth a few moments of sincere conversation. Skillful listening opens stubborn minds, and heals dejected hearts.

4. Teach the basic principle of 'Freedom, not License.'

The one supreme value which we need to learn, teach, and practice is the reverence for all living beings.

Simply: Nobody is allowed to hurt any person or any living thing. This idea is the core principle of the Summerhill School in England, founded by A. S. Neill.

5. Creative Role-Playing (CRP).

Creative Role-Playing is an activity similar to improvisational drama: the players assume roles and act spontaneously, saying and doing whatever they think and feel. Conducted by a skilled leader, CRP becomes a powerful tool for teaching empathy ('feeling-in') and insight ('seeing-in') — to help us to imagine the heart and the mind of another human being.

6. Motivation Techniques.

When we need to inspire children to do something they have not done and something which is genuinely good for them, then there are a number of effective motivation techniques which can be used to inspire children to help themselves.

7. Pedocracy: The Government by Children.

Let the children decide, or let the children work together with you to decide. This participation and this freedom promotes thinking and responsibility. Complete democracy — except for decisions about safety and health — has been the heart of the philosophy of the Summerhill School in England since the school began in 1921.

8. Interpersonal Techniques.

Most problematic behaviors involve interpersonal conflicts, which can be eased with various interpersonal techniques. The common goal of all of these techniques is to heal the damaged relationships between the persons involved.

9. Give the Child a Time-In .

Play with the child, and share a healthy activity together. Nourish the child by providing her with something she genuinely needs: friendship, play, nature, and books and the arts.

Children behave problematically because they lack some basic needs. Fulfilling these needs is the most profound way to treat the immediate situation, and to heal the underlying causes.

10. Intervene Now!
then L. E. N. D. (Listen, Explain, Nourish, Design).

First, the adult must intervene immediately, to stop the endangering problematic behavior. Harmful behavior must be stopped immediately.

Then — Listen, Explain, Nourish with basic needs, and Design a plan to follow up and help the child. After stopping the endangering PB, the parent or child-maintenance worker can help the aggressive child in these four ways:

1) Listen sincerely.

2) Explain why harming others is not permitted.

3) Nourish the child by giving him the opportunity to participate in the creative activities of friendship, play, nature, and the arts.

4) Design a follow-up plan to observe the child, intervene when needed, and continue to nourish with the basic needs. The essence of true caring is to engage in this entire process, to make a complete commitment to helping and healing the aggressive child.

In the upcoming Chapters 5 through 14, we will examine each of these ten techniques, and then employ real-life examples to illustrate how these techniques can be used wisely, creatively, and well.

♥

Chapter 5

Technique # 1: Acceptance

A small pot boils easily.
— Dutch Proverb

Many times in your work with children, the child's behavior might appear to be problematic but actually it is not. In these cases, the best thing to do is to accept the child's actions, do nothing, and refrain from intervening.

Let's examine the case of the cross-eyed teacher who had no control over his pupils. Whenever the students laughed, the teacher shouted in anger "Put your heads down on the desk! Put your heads down!"

This authoritarian indoctrinator — the title of "teacher" or "educator" he does not deserve — did not understand how to determine if the child's behavior is or is not problematic.

The test is to apply the principle of 'Freedom, not License':

"Is the child's behavior harming another person or another living thing?"

And then ask our extended question: "Is the child in need of help?"

Had this instructor laughed with the children, instead of forbidding all laughter, then he might have been able to create a classroom atmosphere of joy, the only kind of classroom where true learning can grow.

An Important Caution About This Technique

There is one important caution we should remember about the Technique of Acceptance. It is **never** appropriate when children are fighting; it is **never** appropriate when the health or safety of the children are at risk. In these cases we must act, and we must act immediately to stop the endangering behavior. How to do this will be explained in future chapters.

The Value of Acceptance

Children want and need to be accepted by grownups. Some have called this acceptance by another name: 'approval.' When we accept ourselves, accept the child, and approve of the child in all moments, then the child can flourish. We may disagree or disapprove of the child's action, but at all times we can accept and approve the child herself.

The Technique of Acceptance is most appropriate when children are not engaging in problematic behavior. Yet acceptance in a deeper sense is much more than a technique, it is a whole philosophy of living. The Chinese Taoists swore by it; Walt Whitman wove his life and his poems around it; and modern psychologists, including E. Graham Howe and Carl Jung both sing its praises to the skies. Acceptance is not Stoic resignation. Acceptance is a way of being which helps to embrace life, and to live with more resilience and more happiness.

Adults who have learned to live this open, accepting philosophy are happy individuals. And one of the best — perhaps the best of all! — gifts we can give to the children we live with and work with is this gift of joy, this sublime gift of happiness shared with another human being.

Responding To Problematic Behavior with The Technique of Acceptance

How does the technique of acceptance work in actual practice?

To answer this question, we will examine an Opportunity-Problem from the book *101 Problems in Child Maintenance*. Like all the Opportunity-Problems in that book, this one happened in real life.

Opportunity-Problem #1. The Wisecracker

A new child joins your group. He's 14 years old, his nickname is 'Toad', and the minute he steps off the bus he swaggers toward you with a troublemaking smirk on his face. He's dressed in army pants, and he has a short-short haircut with the letter 'Z' carved on the side of his head. Toad glares at your bright yellow shirt, and he shouts out: "Hey, bozo, does that shirt glow in the dark?"

The thirty kids standing all around burst out laughing. What do you say and do?

STOP and THINK

Don't jump to the solution!

First, stop to think how you would manage this situation without using force or punishment. Write down your ideas, or discuss this situation with your spouse, relatives, co-workers, or friends. After you have thought thoroughly about it, you may proceed to the conclusion of this chapter.

Solutions to all the Opportunity-Problems are given in Chapter 16.

Notes and Summary for Chapter 5

Problematic behavior has been explained as behavior that harms oneself or others, or situations where a child requires help. When problematic behavior occurs, then the parent or child-maintenance worker must intervene. For situations involving true PB, the nonaction in the technique of Acceptance is not appropriate. Yet for much of the time we spend with children, Acceptance is an essential element for establishing genuine relationships. Parents and child-maintenance workers need to learn how to distinguish between problematic behavior and healthy fun. Relax, laugh more, and let kids behave as kids.

♥

Chapter 6

Technique # 2:
Change The Circumstances

If there is anything we wish to change in the child, we should first examine it and see whether it is not something that could better be changed in ourselves.
— Carl Jung

The Technique of Change the Circumstances — not changing the child's behavior or attitude — is the right response when the child's problematic behavior has been caused by adults. I have called these situations 'adultogenic problems': problems caused by adults. There are many kinds of mistakes we make which cause problematic behavior: too must strictness, unfair rules, excessive punishments, and unnourishing environments. Often in these situations, the right response is to change the circumstances to undo our mistakes, and to accommodate the child's needs.

The Gentle Defiance of Oliver Twist

The everyday life around us is filled with examples of children's problematic behavior caused by adults. In literature, the blatant blunders and bad influences of adults on children has been chronicled brilliantly by Charles Dickens. The celebrated "Please, sir, I want some more," scene in his 1837 novel *Oliver Twist* is a perfect example of our imperfect social world.

After working all the day, the boys in the workhouse have gathered inside their stone-walled dining hall. The typical evening meal — one small bowl of watery gruel — has driven them to hungry hopelessness. The boys draw lots to determine who will ask the unaskable, and the choice falls on Oliver Twist. Oliver, age nine, is meek as a mouse, trusting as angel, skinny as a butter knife.

"Desperate with hunger and reckless with misery," Oliver advances to the master and makes his humble plea: "Please sir, I want some more."

The master was a fat, healthy man; but he turned very pale. He gazed in stupefied astonishment on the small rebel for some seconds, and then clung for support to the copper. The assistants were paralyzed with wonder; the boys with fear.

"What!" said the master at length, in a faint voice.

"Please sir," replied Oliver, "I want some more."

The master aimed a blow at Oliver's head with the ladle; pinioned him in his arms; and shrieked aloud for the beadle.

The board was in the sitting room in solemn conclave, when Mr. Bumble rushed into the room in great excitement, and addressing the gentleman in the high chair, said,

"Mr. Limbkins, I beg your pardon, sir! Oliver Twist has asked for more!"

There was a general start. Horror was depicted on every countenance.

"For more!" said Mr. Limbkins. "Compose yourself, Bumble, and answer me distinctly. Do I understand that he asked for more, after he had eaten the supper allotted by the dietary?"

"He did, sir," replied Bumble.

"That boy will be hung," said the gentleman in the white waistcoat. "I know that boy will be hung."

Poor Oliver! For his honesty and courage he was immediately thrown into solitary confinement, flogged in front of the other boys as a public warning, then offered up as an apprentice to any tradesman who would take him for a bounty of five pounds.

What should have happened instead? Had the child-maintenance worker — the bumbling master Mr. Bumble — read this book, then he could have responded more humanely. He first would have identified this problem as adultogenic, then applied the Technique of Change the Circumstances, then given Oliver — and the other boys — all the food that they required.

When Not To Use and When To Use This Technique

Let's return to the case of the teacher suppressing laughter in the classroom. When children are behaving naturally, when the problems are vitality problems, then usually the right response is to let the children be themselves. No changes are needed, except changes in our own attitude toward more tolerance, patience, and wisdom.

In many other situations involving children, 'change the circumstances' can be combined with other techniques to help children in many ways. For example: instead of forbidding a child (who cannot swim) to enter a swimming pool (as many overprotective mothers do), the child might be allowed to enter the pool only when accompanied one-on-one by a responsible adult. Instead of keeping an infant locked inside a playpen all day, the parents might eliminate the child-unfriendly hazards in their living room.

Adults often cause problematic behavior in children by their use of physical force, threats, or an authoritarian approach. Spanking and corporal punishment, which has been proven to be harmful to children, has been banned in schools in 128 countries (of the 195 countries in our world) and made illegal in 31 of the 50 U.S. states. Other authoritarian approaches — when adults attempt to dominate children by threats and fear — have harmful and unwanted aftereffects. In some cases, children ruled by force become resentful, rebellious, frustrated, and overstressed. In other cases, children become submissive and passive, incapable of self-reliant behavior and thinking independently.

What Are Some of the Many Ways That Adults Cause Children to Behave Problematically?

Here are twelve questions about behaviors and environments of parents and child-maintenance workers that can cause children to act problematically.

In these cases, an excellent response to the problematic behavior — PB caused by these situations — is to Change the Circumstances.

A. Are we neglecting our children, and not spending enough time with our kids?

B. Are we providing children with their basic needs? (see Chapter 23)

C. Are we playing and having fun with our kids?

D. Do we have frequent discussions with our children, where we listen deeply and talk sincerely?

E. Do we hurry-rush children from one place to another, preventing them from entering the timelessly flowing world of childhood?

F. Do we allow — and even encourage — children to spend too much time watching television, playing video games, and hanging out on social media sites?

G. Are we giving children too many possessions, and surrounding their lives with too much comfort and luxury?

H. Are we taking action to reduce violence in our own lives, in the media, in our neighborhoods, and on our planet?

I. With the way we our living our own lives, are we giving children good role models to emulate?

J. Are we using outmoded authoritarian techniques when managing problematic behavior — instead of calm, creative, and caring responses?

K. Are we fixing our schools to make them free from violence, free from authoritarian techniques, and places where students experience the joy of learning?

L. Are we continually learning and improving our child-maintenance skills — the theory and the practice — by reading and by talking with other CMWs?

Responding To Problematic Behavior With The Technique of Change The Circumstances

How does the technique 'Change the Circumstances' work in actual practice?

To answer this question, we will examine an Opportunity-Problem from the book *101 Problems in Child Maintenance*.

Opportunity-Problem # 2. A Homesick Runaway

You wake up early one morning, call your kids together for a meeting, then discover that Hubert (age 10) is missing. Hubert's shelves are empty — he's packed his bags and hit the road. Ten minutes later you find him, walking at turtle speed, carrying a heavy backpack and dragging a weighty duffel bag. He is walking down the main road, heading for the main gate.

CMW: Hubert, why are you running away?"

Hubert (crying with tears): I hate it here! I'm going home!

CMW: How? From here to the city is two-hundred miles.

Hubert: I'm walking.

Hubert keeps on walking, and dragging his baggage toward the gate.

CMW: Hubert, come back with me and we'll talk about it.

No answer.

Hubert walks on.

STOP and THINK

Don't jump to the solution! First, stop to think how you would manage this situation without using force or punishment. Write down your ideas, or discuss this situation with your spouse, relatives, co-workers, or friends. After you have thought thoroughly about it, you may proceed to the conclusion of this chapter. Solutions to all the Opportunity-Problems are given in Chapter 16.

Notes and Summary for Chapter 6

Adults are the cause of much problematic behavior in children. We create problems by our forceful methods, blind faith in punishment, our neglect, our deceptions, or by placing children in inappropriate environments. When we are wise enough to recognize our mistakes, we can help children when we change ourselves and change the circumstances.

> There's a lot of difference between listening and hearing.
>
> — G. K. Chesterton

Listening is a magnetic and strange thing,
a creative force. The friends who listen to us
are the ones we move toward.
When we are listened to, it creates us,
makes us unfold and expand.

— Karl A. Menninger

The most important thing in communication
is hearing what isn't said.

— Peter Drucker

We think we listen, but very rarely do we listen
with real understanding, true empathy.
Yet listening, of this very special kind,
is one of the most potent forces for change that I know.

— Carl Rogers

Chapter 7

Technique # 3
Listening and Talking

A thousand years of shouting is not worth a few moments of sincere conversation. The most stubborn wills, the most closed minds, the most dejected hearts, can be opened and transformed by skillful listening.
— Michael Pastore

If we want a child to listen to us, then first we need to listen to the child. Most grownups listen superficially. Here are four examples of superficial listening followed by automatic replies.

Child: I got into a fight this morning.
Grownup: Can't you ever stay out of trouble?

Child: I hate my history teacher.
Grownup: Why don't you give her a chance?

Child: My pet chameleon died.
Grownup: Death happens. You can get a new pet.

Child: Harry is picking on me.
Grownup: Ignore him and he won't bother you.

Most grownups reply by
→ criticizing
→ talking too much
→ talking about themselves
→ making snap judgements
→ giving automatic answers
→ answering a different question
→ spewing platitudinous advice.

What is wrong with this kind of listening? It is not true listening at all. The grownup bombards the child with criticisms or advice. His habitual and hackneyed replies chop off the conversation like a guillotine. The child never gets the chance to fully express his feelings. Dialogue never grows.

The genuine way to listen is an experience which I have called 'Listening Deep.' Listening Deep means listening without criticizing; without making judgments; without offering stock answers and clichés; without trying to convince someone of something; without trying to change the other person's feelings or ideas. When we listen deeply, we listen with our profoundest concentration; we listen with the depths of our whole being; we listen caringly. We hear the words and we feel the supercharged emotions underneath the words. And then we respond to the child with our deepest sincerity, compassion, insight, and empathy.

What's the result of this variety of listening? ... The child is allowed to talk more, to listen to her own feelings, and to figure out solutions for herself.

When Not To Use and When To Use
The Technique Of Listening and Talking

Listening and Talking is not the right technique in those moments when we need to act immediately to prevent a child from harming himself or another person. After the danger from these situations has passed, listening and talking is both good and necessary.

Listening and talking is a great all-purpose technique that works well with almost every type of problematic behavior. When children are experiencing personal problems — fears, struggles of conscience, confusion about relationships, stress over conflict with others — then listening and talking is the best way to help and heal.

For listening and talking to be most effective, the proper time and place is needed. When children are angry or upset, or when the parent or child-maintenance worker is upset — these are not good times to talk. First calm yourself then calm the child, then ask the child if she would like to talk with you.

Many listening situations — especially when the subject revolves around personal problems — should be conducted in private, away from the ears of other children.

Sometimes, the best time to talk about a situation is immediately during or after the problematic event occurs.

At other times, it is good to remember the acronym 'INTAIL': Ignore Now, Talk About It Later.

Listening and talking are best conducted in a place free from distractions, interruptions, and eavesdroppers.

The ancient Greek way of talk-as-you-walk assures privacy, and contributes to good health.

Socrates Reborn:
How To Listen With A Group Of Children

Talking and listening with a group of children is most effective when it is conducted in the spirit of Socrates. The rivals of Socrates, called the Sophists, pretended that they had absolute knowledge. Whenever they talked, they argued: they attempted to convince their listeners that their (the Sophists) points of view were right and indisputable and true.

Socrates invented a better way. When Socrates engaged someone in conversation, he behaved as if they were partners, working together in the noble search for truth. "If you can show me that you are right," said Socrates, "then I will be the first to give way."

Enter into your discussions with children in the Socratic spirit of working together to find the best way for problems to be resolved. You will be astounded how effective this method can be. Sessions of genuine listening-and-talking open up young minds, and become true models of cooperation, participation, and honesty.

Responding To Problematic Behavior
With The Technique of Listening and Talking

Here is a typical example of problematic behavior which can be effectively healed by using the technique of Listening and Talking.

Opportunity-Problem # 3. Trouble at Home

David, age 9, who has not spoken one word all day, at last says to the child-maintenance worker:

"My father yells at my mother all the time and I think he's crazy."

After this confession, the child sinks back into sulky silence.

STOP and THINK

Don't jump to the solution! First, stop to think how you would manage this situation without using force or punishment. Write down your ideas, or discuss this situation with your spouse, relatives, co-workers, or friends. (To benefit most from this exercise, write your solution as a dialogue between the listening-deep child-maintenance worker and the troubled David.) After you have thought thoroughly about it, you may proceed to the conclusion of this chapter.

Solutions to all the Opportunity-Problems are given in Chapter 16.

Notes and Summary for Chapter 7

The Technique of Listening and Talking is a simple, natural, and powerful method for building a rapport with other persons, and for resolving almost every variety of problematic behavior. A good listener is rare. And genuine listening is an art which requires courage, patience, practice, concentration. Whenever Listening Deep takes place, both persons are transformed. Listening is the way great friendships are made. For with our true friends we can speak with complete openness, happy in the knowledge that our real self is always accepted, appreciated, encouraged, and approved.

♥

Chapter 8

Technique # 4:
Teach 'Freedom, not License.'

Now I see the secret of making the best persons,
It is to grow in the open air and to eat and sleep with the
earth.
— Walt Whitman

The one supreme value which we need to learn, to teach,
and to practice is the reverence for all living beings.
Simply: No one is allowed to hurt any person or any
living thing. You are free to do what you like, but you are
not free to interfere with another person's freedom, and
you are not free to harm another person or living thing.
This abuse of freedom is what A. S. Neill calls: 'license.'

This chapter explains the whys, whens, and the hows
about teaching this basic principle of human relations:
'Freedom, not License.'

When Not To Use and When To Use
The Technique of Teach 'Freedom, Not License'

Like many of our other techniques, when urgent
action is required — when the health or safety of a child is

immediately in danger — then in that moment what needs to be done is to take action, not to stop to talk and teach. And obviously, this teaching is ineffective when children are angry or otherwise extremely upset.

In those moments, the first step is to protect the child from danger, then to calm the child — not to barrage him with words, words, words.

To prevent problems, or to respond to problems that have happened once, teaching 'Freedom not License' is often a very good option. When children harm each other or nonhuman living beings, or when children interfere with the freedom of another person — then the time is all-ripe for teaching this essential theme.

One Great Obstacle To the Technique
Teach 'Freedom, not License'

Our 21st Century culture is permeated with violence in deeds and in words. Our streets are violent. Our sports are violent. Our political talk is violent. And even our entertainments — films, television programs, social media sites, and video games — are rife with hostility, aggression, and threats to harm.

Children learn by imitation. Children absorb whatever models the society makes available to them. Once a week from his parent the child hears "Don't hit!" — but hundreds of times and even thousands of times per week the same child watches well-paid actors splattering blood and blasting bodies everywhere.

It is urgent that we reduce the amount of televised violence, and computer-game violence, which assaults the senses of our children. We do not need to wait until the media moguls transform their industries. Parents and child-maintenance workers can — and must — restrict the child's exposure to these harmful and wasteful activities right now.

When we protect our children from viewing violence, we open the door to the voices of nonviolence, genuine caring, and healthy human relationships.

Cutting down or eliminating the child's time spent with violent entertainments is the first step toward teaching the higher values which all human beings require for social harmony and personal happiness.

Four Ideas About How To Teach This Technique

Here are four ways to teach children about this theme:
A. Teach by example
B. Teach by contact with nature
C. Teach by talking together
D. Teach by telling and reading great stories and books.

A. Teach by Example: Gandhi's Tooth

The life and words of Mahatma Gandhi (1869–1948) — who taught that "All men are brothers." — offer a wealth of wisdom and inspiration for everyone. Gandhi did what all truly great persons do: he lived his vision, and then he spoke from own experience. Before preaching to others, Gandhi would first live the truth himself. Long before Albert Schweitzer coined this motto,

Gandhi practiced these essential words: "Teaching by example is not the best way to teach. It is the only way."

Here is one of many stories about this remarkable man.

A mother of a young child visited Mahatma Gandhi to ask advice. The mother said:

"My child is eating too much sugar. Please tell me what to do." Gandhi answered: "Come back in three days."

Three days later the mother returned. Gandhi smiled to her and said:

"Now tell your child to stop eating sugar."

Curious, the mother asked: "Why did you need to wait three days to tell me to tell my son to stop eating sugar?"

Gandhi replied: "I had a sweet tooth. It took me three days to stop eating sugar."

Children — grownups also — learn by imitating the parents and child-maintenance workers around them. Parents and child-maintenance workers who are respectful of other persons and other living beings will teach more by example than by all the world's words.

B. Teach by Contact With Nature

In *The Terrestrial Gospel of Nikos Kazantzakis*, the poet/translator Thanasis Maskaleris writes: "The gifts of the Earth, as Kazantzakis depicts them, are boundless: there is the great joy of the senses, the heart and the soul, as they take in her beauty; then there is her gift of sustaining all living things, and sustaining all growth."

All living beings are connected. The child's development into a loving and fulfilled human being depends largely on her relationship with nature. If nature matters in her life, then the child will be continually renewed by the wisdom of the wild: she will learn simple living, peacefulness within, and the deep happiness that comes from caring about something outside of herself.

How can the parent or child-maintenance worker help in these great tasks? ... First and last, by leading the children to enjoy Nature. Children who deeply enjoy living, working, and playing in the outdoors will never lose their sense of wonder. And children who wonder and delight in wild places will grow to grasp the most important of all ideas: reverence for life.

There is no need for complex lesson plans: Nature herself is the great and endless book. Thanks to their inborn compassion and love, children will learn naturally to respect and to care for all living beings. All we need to do is to provide the opportunities.

C. Teach by Talking Together

Are people in our fast-paced culture talking to each other? Really talking? ... Many recently-published books answer that question with a definite "No!" Many adults have let themselves become too busy to take time for talking to one another. When we do talk it is usually about trivia: sports, news, factoids, money, things we can buy. Bombarded by commercial sound bytes, we are losing the capacity to discern what is significant and what is not.

Yet words spoken from the heart about our inmost experiences and ideals can often penetrate beneath the surface and move us in mysterious ways. The whole key is sincerity.

A sincere discussion about things that matter, for example:
- respect for all human beings
- respect all living beings living beings
- the rights of animals
- the importance of vegetarianism
- why we should respect ourselves and other persons
- why we want to leave a wilderness area at least as pristine as before we entered.

These simple truths will make a deep impression on most children. And these ideas have the power to stay with the children for years and years to come. Children understand this kinship with all beings, and discussing these ideas corroborates the truths they already feel and deeply know.

D. Teach by Reading Stories and Books

Literature began with stories and myths which preserved and transmitted the values and ideals of the whole culture.

Most books published today are absent of profound values and ideas. But the great books still survive to teach us, and to help us to survive. To encourage children to read the best books is to open them to worlds which will inspire them with awe, wonder, compassion, integrity, and courage to act.

The way to do this is so simple: just make time in every day for reading the best books. Parents or child-maintenance workers might read to the children, or tell stories to the children, and also to keep books in easy-to-get places, so that children can read the books when they are alone.

Which books are mind-opening? ... See Appendixes A and C for two excellent lists: one list of books and stories for children, and another list of books for adults.

Responding To Problematic Behavior
With The Technique of Teach 'Freedom, Not License'

Here is a typical example of problematic behavior which can be effectively healed by using this technique.

Opportunity-Problem # 4. Tattooing Trees

Billy, age 10, has just carved "Billy loves Cleopatra!" into the bark of an old oak tree. When the child-maintenance worker Ben asked Billy:

"Why did you carve the tree bark?"

Billy answered: "Because I felt like it."

What should the child-maintenance worker do now?

STOP and THINK

Don't jump to the solution! First, stop to think how you would manage this situation without using force or punishment. Write down your ideas, or discuss this situation with your spouse, relatives, co-workers, or friends. After you have thought thoroughly about it, you may proceed to the conclusion of this chapter.

Solutions to all the Opportunity-Problems are given in Chapter 16.

Notes and Summary for Chapter 8

For thousands of years philosophers have argued over the question: "Can character be taught?". We don't need to debate the answer in order to teach children the one value which all intelligent and compassionate persons agree upon: Every person has the right to remain free from harm. The task of educators in the future will be to learn how to live and to teach this idea, then to extend this concept to include all living beings. And some educators might even say that to begin by teaching the sacredness of all living beings is the best way to teach persons to respect other humans.

If you believe that every person, and every living being, has the right to live and to remain free from harm, then teach this value to the children in your care. This value may be summarized in the short phrase: 'Freedom, not License.' My personal experience has shown me that children respond with the greatest interest, insight, and enthusiasm to this beautiful wisdom of the heart.

♥

Chapter 9

Technique # 5: Creative Role-Playing

Could a greater miracle take place than for us
to look through each other's eyes for an instant?
— Henry David Thoreau, *Journals*

Creative Role-Playing (CRP) is an activity for all ages, similar to improvisational drama. To play, the players assume roles and then act spontaneously, saying and doing whatever they think and feel. Conducted by a skilled leader, this technique becomes a powerful tool for teaching empathy ('feeling-in') and insight ('seeing-in') — to help us to imagine the heart and the mind of another human being.

When Not To Use and When To Use
The Technique of Creative Role-Playing

Creative Role-Playing is not a technique that can be used for "real-time" problematic behavior — PB which happens in front of your eyes.

The strength of the technique of CRP lies in its power for increasing understanding and awareness. Thus, it is best used either to prevent problems from occurring for the first time, or to resolve problems which have the awful potential to repeat themselves again and again and again.

"To be human," writes Ashley Montagu, "is to be in danger."

For problematic behavior concerning the child's health and safety, Creative Role-Playing can play a vital role. We need to supervise children as much as possible, yet we cannot be with them, or watch them, for all of the 1,440 minutes every day. We cannot cross every street with the children in our care; we cannot brush every tooth; we cannot be always at their side to remind them to be alert, mindful, aware.

And of course, this should not be our goal: our goal is to help children to become self-reliant, to learn how they can take care of themselves. Role-playing in situations where health and safety are involved can help children to be alert, to take precautions, to look before they leap, and to think before they act impulsively.

A Very Important Note About Role-Playing

Creative Role-Playing is a form of play, and it works best when it is done playfully. Parents and children should give role-players an emotional atmosphere that is lighthearted, friendly, and encouraging. Children's participation in role-playing should always be voluntary. The parent (or child-maintenance worker) may ask and encourage, but he should never force the child to participate in role-playing.

How To Use The Technique of Creative Role-Playing

The four phases of Creative Role-Playing are:
1) The Briefing
2) The Role-Playing
3) The Performance
4) The Discussion.

1) The Briefing

Explain to your kids what role-playing is:

Role-playing is pretending to be a unique person in a specific situation.

After this explanation
- ask for questions, then
- select a situation to role-play, then
- describe the person(s) and the situation vividly and concisely.

You can use our book of problematic behavior situations — *101 Problems in Child Maintenance.* Or you can make up your own scenarios. After you and the children have role-played a few of these Opportunity-Problems, ask the kids to invent their imaginary situations. At last, when the kids feel comfortable with role-playing, with you, and with one another — then you can begin using the role-playing situations from the everyday real life around you.

2) The Role-Playing

Now divide the kids into small groups of 2 or 3, or as many characters as required for the dramatic situation. Lights, camera, action, ready, set, role-play! The role-playing is acting: the kids make-pretend that they are someone else. In their roles, players should talk and act with their sincerest feelings and their deepest imagination.

3) The Performance

After the kids have role-played the situation in small groups, the parent or child-maintenance worker asks for volunteers: "Who would like to role-play the situation in front of the whole group?"

Parents or child-maintenance workers who are new to role-playing will probably want to simply sit back and watch the kids perform. Experienced and inventive CRP leaders will be able to intervene at the right moments, to add humor and drama to the session.

4) The Discussion

After the action, the parent or child-maintenance workers and the whole group of kids should discuss the dramas just performed. Children should be encouraged to compare their before-and-after viewpoints about the situation. Ask the child: "What new ideas, feelings, and insights have you gained?"

Responding To Problematic Behavior With
The Technique of Creative Role-Playing

Here is a sample opportunity-problem to solve using Creative Role-Playing. Read the problem below, then before you peek at the answer — write down how the role-playing session might proceed.

Opportunity-Problem # 5. Vanishing Kids

You've asked your kids to go straight to the theater for drama class, and the moment they leave you they are suspiciously smiling. Twenty minutes later the drama teacher, Otto, rushes at you melodramatically, waves his arms, and then demands to know where your children are. You search and search and search.

Thirty minutes later you find the kids, having a great time, laughing and running barefoot in the creek.

STOP and THINK

Don't jump to the solution! First, stop to think how you would manage this situation without using force or punishment. Write down your ideas, or discuss this situation with your spouse, relatives, co-workers, or friends. After you have thought thoroughly about it, you may proceed to the conclusion of this chapter.

Solutions to all the Opportunity-Problems are given in Chapter 16.

Notes and Summary for Chapter 9

Creative Role-Playing is a versatile and powerful technique because it increases awareness and appreciation of others, and in one activity combines learning and enjoyment.

When we work with children we often attempt to teach and help them in two realms: the child's behavior and the child's attitude. Of course, these elements are naturally interconnected. Creative Role-Playing, with its focus on encouraging empathy, is a valuable technique for opening the child's attitudes toward healthier and happier perspectives.

Chapter 10

Technique # 6:
Motivation Techniques

Student: Good morning, Teacher. Would you punish me
for something I didn't do?
Teacher: No, of course not!
Student: Good! I didn't do my homework assignment!

Good parenting and good 'child-maintenance working'
does not consist in forcing children, or even in convincing
children, to do what we want them to do. Good parenting
and child-maintenance working begins when we
understand what is truly good for the child. When we
need to inspire a child to do something he has not done
which is genuinely good for him — then the techniques of
motivation are an excellent choice.

When Not To Use and When To Use
the Motivation Techniques

Let us imaginatively return to that bleary stone dining
hall in London, and to our young friend Oliver Twist. You
remember (in Charle's Dickens's eponymous novel, and

in this book's Chapter 6) that Oliver was punished after he humbly requested more food.

Now suppose that Oliver's child-maintenance workers had been more wily. Instead of suppressing the rebellion of Oliver and his ravenous friends by force, they might have attempted to do so by motivation and persuasion. They might have sworn — as their modern political counterparts would swear — that there is no budget for more food, and without money there is nothing that can be done. They might have attempted to persuade the boys to be satisfied with, or even thankful for, their meager portions.

This approach is blatantly unjust; I have included it here merely to illustrate a point about when the techniques of motivation never should be used. Motivation Techniques should never be used to move the child toward goals which are not good for him or good for the entire group. In those cases, motivation turns sour as it turns into those powerful weapons we call manipulation and propaganda.

What situations call for the use of motivation techniques?

Use these techniques whenever the child or group of children have not done something that needs to be done — but first make certain that the action you are motivating the child to do is genuinely good for this child.

Motivation Is Not Bribery
and Bribery is Not Motivation

In the fine book by Gabor Maté, *Scattered: How Attention Deficit Disorder Originates And What You Can Do About It* — Dr. Maté writes:

"It is worth recalling here that the injudicious use of rewards and praise can be pressure tactics no less than verbal or physical coercion."

Rewarding or bribing children with money, or with stars which can be redeemed for presents, is not at all what we have in mind. Like punishments, material rewards are often used by parents and child-maintenance workers because they are convenient, time-saving, and require no thinking to apply.

What about in the long run:
Do rewards work?

I believe that they do not. There are many arguments against using rewards to influence a child's behavior. The strongest of these is this one: rewards encourage children for the wrong reasons.

Compare these two cases and note well the difference. In Case 1, Harry brushes his teeth every morning because when he does, he gets a star worth ten cents. What does this teach Harry? That the reason to do something is to make money. Will Harry brush his teeth when no one is around to dole out stars? The answer to this is obvious.

In Case 2, Julie brushes her teeth because she wants to avoid cavities and halitosis, and she desires to have healthy teeth and an attractive smile. Whether or not the reward is available, each morning and each evening Julie will brush her teeth thoroughly — she will brush the three surfaces of each tooth ten times.

The Many Ways To Motivate Children

Here is a list and a brief description of my ten favorite ways to motivate kids. Parents and child-maintenance workers can choose any of these that might apply to their child's problematic behavior. If one doesn't do the job, then try another and another, until you find the one which works.

6.1 :: Share Your Enthusiasm.

In this method, you genuinely enjoy doing something and you inspire children with your wholehearted enthusiasm.

6.2 :: Lead By Example.

As Albert Schweitzer remarked: "Teaching by example is not the best way to teach. It is the only way."

6.3 :: Use Humor.

Using humor with children is better than a magic charm.

6.4 :: Make It Fun or Make It A Game.

Mary Poppins, in the movie *Mary Poppins*, knew the secret of this one when she sang: "In every job which must be done there is an element of fun, you find the fun and snap! the job's a game."

6.5 :: Let Kids Participate in Making Decisions and Plans.

Have the foresight to allow children to work with you to plan activities which involve them. Whenever kids participate in the planning, their motivation will be much higher than if the parent or child-maintenance worker has planned the activity alone. For details about this technique, see Chapter 11 and the discussion of pedocracy.

6.6 :: Offer Fun Alternatives (OFA).

A simple and amazingly effective way to help children to focus on the activities that are both fun and good for them. A laughing, running, hiding, chasing game of Spring Tag is a thousand times more fun than an hour in front of the TV.

6.7 :: Ask Kids To Help Other Kids.

Whenever you can involve kids in the process of helping other children, then everyone involved is educated and helped. (This is also an Interpersonal Technique, which will be discussed in more detail in Chapter 12.)

6.8 :: Give Nonmaterial Rewards.

This method should be utilized carefully, so that it is not confused with bribes. For example, a shrewd parent or child-maintenance worker might say: "This room is a mess and I need to clean it up, and that's going to take one hour. If only I had some help and the room could be cleaned up sooner, then I would be free to take you kids to the park."

6.9 :: Use Reason To Explain How and Why Your Mutual Goal is Worthwhile.

An intelligent child, from age six onward, can understand that some actions are helpful to him, and some are harmful. The humble torch of reason has lighted many paths of happiness.

6.10 :: Discover and Remove The Root Of The Problem.

This is always the best solution to every problem. If you can understand why the child isn't doing what is good for him to do, then you can often solve the problem by the simplest means.

Responding To Problematic Behavior
With the Motivation Techniques

Once you've identified the problem as the type that can be resolved by using motivation, then you need to choose and apply one of the ten motivation techniques above, or other techniques which you invent. Here below is a case to practice on. Read this opportunity-problem, then — before you look at the answer — select a motivation technique that you think would be appropriate.

Opportunity-Problem # 6. Slimy Teeth

You've been living with Melvin for 4 days, and you've just noticed that Melvin's toothbrush is still brand new, and his toothpaste has never been opened.

His teeth are covered with a film of extra-terrestrial yellow-green slime.

Child-maintenance worker: Melvin, have you brushed your teeth for the last four days?

Melvin: No.

Child-maintenance worker: Go brush your teeth right now. If you don't brush, you'll get cavities and your teeth will hurt, then they'll all fall out.

Melvin: If my teeth fall out, then they won't hurt anymore and I won't have to brush.

Child-maintenance worker: Go brush your teeth. Now.

Melvin: No.

What should the child-maintenance worker say and do?

STOP and THINK

Don't jump to the solution! First, stop to think how you would manage this situation without using force or punishment. Write down your ideas, or discuss this situation with your spouse, relatives, co-workers, or friends. After you have thought thoroughly about it, you may proceed to the conclusion of this chapter. Solutions to all the Opportunity-Problems are given in Chapter 16.

Notes and Summary for Chapter 10

Motivation techniques should never be attempted unless we can answer 'Yes!' to question 1 ("the motivation question") and "No!" to question 2, below:

1. Is the goal — the behavior we want the child to begin — a worthwhile goal, genuinely good for the individual child, or good for the group of children?

2. Is the goal to make life easier for the adult, or to impose the adult's authority and power?

When the goal is to help the child, not to deceive him, then using one of the many motivation techniques can often resolve opportunity-problems with amazing speed.

As with every problematic behavior, the power of the technique increases whenever the parent or child-maintenance worker and the child already have established a sincere friendship and rapport. ♥

Chapter 11

Technique # 7:
Pedocracy:
The Government By Children

As I would not be a slave, so I would not be a master.
This expresses my idea of democracy.
— Abraham Lincoln (1809—1865)

There are two facets to the Technique of Pedocracy. One is a government by children, where children meet on a regular basis and make the rules they believe in. There is another equally effective way to use this technique: the parent or child-maintenance worker can enlist the help of a group children to resolve a problem. In both cases, the children work together with the parent or child-maintenance worker to devise a solution acceptable to everyone involved.

This participation and this freedom promotes thinking and responsibility. Except for decisions about safety and health, pedocracy has been a cornerstone of the philosophy of the Summerhill School in England since they opened in the year 1921. This noble experiment in self-government has been a true democracy, where each child and each staff member at Summerhill holds one equal vote. The meetings are used not only to decide school policies and rules, but also to resolve all varieties of conflicts and problematic behavior.

Can children govern themselves, and take responsibility for their own behavior? ... When I was a boy, the streets and the playgrounds in my city were filled with children playing games together, without adult supervision and without adult rules. When disputes arose in a game of sports, they were talked about then resolved quickly. After these healthy conflicts, the games continued with enjoyment and good feelings. In the most difficult situations, when an agreement could not be reached, everyone agreed on what we called a 'do-over' — just go back and play the play again.

When Not To Use and When To Use the Technique of Pedocracy

Obviously, when the need to act immediately is urgent — when there's a fight in progress, or when a child or children are in danger — we cannot pause to convene a meeting of the minds: we cannot use this pedocratic technique. Another time not to use pedocracy is when the problematic behavior is a personal problem, too embarrassing to reveal to the entire group.

When can pedocracy be used? Pedocracy is especially effective when resolving conflicts which arise about money, material possessions, and property. Except for the exceptions noted in the paragraph above, pedocracy works well with just about every other type of problematic behavior.

Why is pedocracy so effective? Firstly, children usually give very good advice. Secondly, children will be much more willing to accept and adhere to the decisions of their peers. Thirdly, it allows the parent or child-maintenance worker and child to remain on friendly terms, and still get the problems solved. And fourthly, children who govern themselves learn to be self-reliant and more responsible for their actions.

How Pedocracy Works

As mentioned above, the best thriving example of the government by children occurs in weekly meetings at Summerhill School. All members of the Summerhill community gather every Thursday night to enact, revoke, or revise their rules, and to resolve any interpersonal problems which anyone chooses to bring up. Each member of the school — from the child age six to the adult teaching staff — holds one equal vote. If Joey has broken a window screen and somebody complains about it, then the group may propose a consequence, for example, that Joey needs to repair the window or pay for the repair. For a detailed description of these meetings, see the book *Summerhill School: a New View of Childhood* by A. S. Neill.

Be Careful When Using the Technique of Pedocracy

The children at Summerhill School practice pedocracy every day, and so they learn to do it well — with fairness for everyone. To offer this option to a typical group of American children, who are accustomed to being told what to do, might be a serious mistake. These children will be unequipped to decide fairly, and might dish out harsh punishments to other children. They might treat other children the same way that punitive adults have treated them. Many children who have been reared under tyranny can imagine no other way.

Parents and child-maintenance workers can never allow children to be cruel or unfair to other children. Does this mean that we cannot use the Technique of Pedocracy? ... We can use the technique, but like all powerful tools, it must be used with caution, supervision, and good judgment.

I have used this technique very successfully with what I call OMY, "Ours, Mine, and Yours." I tell the children that some of the group decisions will be Ours — decisions we make together, worked out to everyone's satisfaction. Some decisions will be all Mine (the child-maintenance worker's), and some decisions will be all Yours — decisions made by the children.

As the children's skill in discussion and fairness increases, and as they shed the "do-it-or-else!" notions learned from foolish teachers and parents — then, gradually, I can increase the quantity and the variety of situations that the children can discuss, and then make decisions about.

A Very Important Note About Health and Safety

Here is a very important note: All decisions about health and safety must be decided by the adults. Children may vote about decisions in every other realm but these.

Responding To Problematic Behavior With The Technique of Pedocracy

How does the technique of pedocracy work in actual practice?

To answer this question, we will examine another interesting Opportunity-Problem from the paperback book *101 Problems in Child Maintenance.*

Opportunity-Problem # 7. A Broken Racket

Without asking permission, David (age 14) borrowed a tennis racket from Mark (age 14). When David returned the racket to Mark, it was smashed and broken beyond repair. Mark is angry. He wants David to pay him one hundred dollars for the racket. David, who comes from a very poor family, hasn't got one dollar, and he resolutely refuses to pay. David says that the racket broke by accident, and that it would have broken no matter who had been using it. Mark asks the child-maintenance worker to make David pay.

STOP and THINK

Don't jump to the solution! First, stop to think how you would manage this situation without using force or punishment. Write down your ideas, or discuss this situation with your spouse, relatives, co-workers, or friends. After you have thought thoroughly about it, you may proceed to the conclusion of this chapter.

Solutions to all the Opportunity-Problems are given in Chapter 16.

Notes and Summary for Chapter 11

Using the Technique of Pedocracy as often as possible will help to resolve conflicts fairly and without violence. In addition, the continual practice of this technique will teach children how to think, how to be fair, and how to be responsible members of a social group.

♥

Chapter 12

Technique # 8: Interpersonal Techniques

The truth must be spoken lovingly.
— Henry David Thoreau

Most problematic behaviors involve interpersonal conflicts, which can be eased with various interpersonal techniques. The common goal for all these techniques is to heal the damaged relationships between the persons involved.

Many of the techniques we have already examined might be defined as 'interpersonal.' The most universal and powerful of these — Listening and Talking — has been discussed in Chapter 7. In this chapter we will explore this and seven additional methods for healing conflicts and resolving problematic behavior.

Conflicts often arise between
- one child versus another child
- one child verus two or more children
- one child versus her parent or child-maintenance worker
- one parent or child-maintenance worker versus her/his group of kids.

When Not To Use and When To Use
Interpersonal Techniques

The 8 Interpersonal Techniques (described below) are not appropriate for removing a child from immediate danger; or for helping a child to solve her personal problems. Instead, these techniques are designed to address the wide range of problematic behaviors where a damaged relationship is the underlying cause.

Eight Interpersonal Techniques

Here are 8 interpersonal techniques which can be used by themselves, or used together with other techniques.
8.1) Ask Eva (A.S.K. E.V.A.)
8.2) The 'We Technique'
8.3) The Helping-Child
8.4) The Technique of Good Deeds
8.5) The Peacemaker
8.6) The Fickle Finger of Fortune
8.7) Repair By Rapport
8.8) Sincere Listening and Talking

8.1 Ask Eva (A.S.K. E.V.A.)

How many problems could be quickly resolved if — without anger and with cheerfulness — we simply asked? For asking to be effective, CMWs need to explain some nourishing activities which the child could do as an alternative to the problematic behavior.

One of the biggest mistakes we make is to tell a child to stop doing something without showing the child a better way. If the child does stop the problematic behavior, then quickly he may begin to engage in a different variety or nuance of PB. Telling kids, "Stop that!" teaches nothing. Instead, we should explain and show some positive alternatives.

A.S.K. E.V.A. stands for:

Ask to Stop Kindly, then Explain Viable Alternatives

This technique is based upon an important concept in teaching. I call this APT: the Axiom of Positive Teaching.

- Use positive speech and teach alternatives.
- It is better to **teach what to do,** than to tell the child what not to do.

For example, during a baseball game, the child is holding the bat on the very bottom of the handle. This is good for some players but not good for everyone, because when held on the very bottom, the bat feels heavier. Many players 'choke up' on the bat, meaning that they move their hands higher up to get a lighter bat and better control. To explain this to the child, you might say:

"Don't hold your hands on the bottom of the bat."

This negative formulation might leave the child bewildered: where should he put his hands?

Much better is to use positive speech and say:

"Move your hands higher up on the bat handle."

The same theme applies to talking about problematic behavior. If you say:

"Stop throwing that ball against the wall!" then the child might obey you — and then throw the ball through a glass window pane.

It is much better to explain an alternative:

"Joey, I don't want that window to break. Let's go out to the field and play catch."

When the child is behaving problematically, try ASK EVA. To apply this technique, just cheerfully and calmly ask the child to stop doing the problematic behavior, then give examples of other activities that the child might want to begin to do.

8.2 The 'We Technique'

The 'We Technique' is a method for responding to problematic behavior that lets the child (or children) help the child-maintenance worker to solve the problem. The child-maintenance worker calmly says to the child (or to the children):

"We have a problem. What can we do to solve it?"

Sharing the responsibility for the solution makes worlds of difference. When the rapport between the child and the child-maintenance worker (or parent) has been a good one, the child will not be shy or afraid to suggest viable solutions. When the rapport is not so friendly, then the child-maintenance worker (or parent) might offer some suggestions, then afterward encourage the child to offer her own ideas. If the child still cannot suggest any ideas, then the next technique might be used in conjunction with this one.

8.3 The Helping-Child

The two false notions which have been eroding modern education and parenting are these: Children and adults must always be at war; and Children are not savvy enough to learn how to manage their own actions. As soon as we disregard these antiquated myths, we can make progress in our own relationships with kids.

This technique is gracefully simple: when one child has a problem, we find another child who is willing and able to help. Sometimes this child will be a friend of the child who is behaving problematically; other times the helper may be older than the child requiring help. In either case, we should never force the child we want to help to accept intervention from other children. But usually this help will be welcomed. After the match has been made and the children have talked together, then the children can meet with the parent or child-maintenance worker, and then work together to resolve the problematic behavior. The 'We Technique' described above, if it failed earlier because the child was silent, might be highly successful at this point.

8.4 The Technique of Good Deeds

One of the most remarkable nonfiction books I've ever studied is *The Ways and Power of Love*, written by

Pitirim A. Sorokin. Sorokin established an institute of altruism at Harvard University, and attempted to discover how altruism could be spread throughout our culture. In one amazing experiment, Sorokin asked a group of subjects to follow these directions.

(Author's Note: Although I am paraphrasing these instructions, the ideas and the results are accurate. —MP)

1) Write down the names of a number of persons you know, whose relationship with you could be accurately described as hostile or antagonistic.

2) Select the one person on this list to whom this sentence applies most certainly: "Nothing at all could be done to improve our relationship and make it less antagonistic."

Then Sorokin instructed his volunteer subjects to begin a campaign of doing good deeds to the person who they named. They might write a note; send a book or a very small gift; say a few kind words — any good deed that they would choose to do.

The results of this unique experiment were overwhelmingly positive. In all cases, the relationships improved significantly. At first, the attitude of the subjects (the good-deed-doers) improves. Then, soon after, there came a noticeable improvement in the attitude of the persons who received the good deeds. Often, the original receivers became givers, and the two persons continued to exchange good deeds with each other. In some cases, close friendships were formed from relationships which had formerly been described as hopelessly antagonistic.

I have used this technique many times with children who said that they hated each other, and said much worse than that.

I would say to the kids:

"Boys and girls, there was a very smart professor who wanted to solve this problem: What can we do when two people are not getting along with each other? ... He asked the people who disliked each other to do something nice for the other person. Can we try that experiment now?"

With great curiosity and enthusiasm, the children agreed. And just as in the Sorokin studies, every time this technique was utilized with my groups of children, relationships improved. Surprisingly, after just a few weeks of mutual good deeds, many sworn enemies were transformed into lasting friends.

8.5 The Peacemaker

When adults cannot resolve conflicts, they at times seek a mediator, or arbitrator, who will decide. This method can be used for resolving conflicts with children, but only if both children agree beforehand to using this process, and agree to the choice of the one Peacemaking Person that they both will trust. The Peacemaker may be either a parent, a child-maintenance worker, or a child. The decision of this Peacemaker should be followed without too much complaint. A caution here: the adult must ensure that the decision of the Peacemaker is not cruel, harmful, inappropriate, or thoroughly unfair.

8.6 The Fickle Finger of Fortune

Here's a quick and simple technique that will work if it's done right. Suppose that David finds a dollar and Jennifer insists it is the dollar that she lost. Jennifer admits, though, that she has no way to prove her claim, and in fact she is not 100 per cent certain that this particular dollar is her missing buck.

If David and Jennifer agree to risk 'the Fickle Finger of Fortune', then the scenario would unfold in this way. The child-maintenance worker takes four small pieces of paper, numbers them from 1 to 4, then writes down the solutions proposed by David and Jennifer. Two of Jennifer's solutions go into the hat, and two of David's solutions.

Here's the tricky catch. Both children must agree that if any of the solutions are selected then they will follow them; and the child-maintenance worker helps the children to generate four possible solutions which they will agree to follow. Thus, all the options are options that both persons are willing to accept.

For example, these are four possible solutions to the problem:

1) Jennifer is believed and she gets to keep the whole dollar.

2) the children split the dollar and each one gets fifty cents.

3) the whole dollar will be donated to charity.

4) a team of children-detectives will be selected to investigate if, in fact, the dollar once belonged to Jennifer.

Next, the child-maintenance worker closes his eyes, puts his fickle finger into the hat, and then pulls out one of these four slips of paper. Whichever solution is pulled out is the one that will be done.

This method can save lots of discussion time. But it works if and only if the children who are involved are satisfied with all the possible outcomes which might result from leaving things to luck.

8.7 Repair By Rapport

Underlying many problem types is the problem of human relationships: in some way the persons involved are failing one another in the realms of appreciation and respect. When we use the technique of 'Repair by Rapport', then we focus on the people aspect, and postpone the problem for a later time.

For example: Billy and Arnold are angry at each other because at a baseball game, Billy got excited and accidentally knocked Arnold's hot dog onto the dirty ground. The parent or child-maintenance worker, instead of rehashing that triggering incident, might decide to focus his energies on healing the break between the persons, Billy and Arnold. To do this, the parent or child-maintenance worker could use any or many of the techniques already discussed in the chapters above. After the interpersonal situation has improved, then the incident will become either nothing at all to worry about, or shrunk to a size so small that it can be treated with ease.

8.8 Sincere Listening and Talking

We have already discussed this extremely important interpersonal technique in Chapter 7. Therefore, here we will add a few more ideas only.

Martin Buber is a philosopher with a theory of interpersonal relationships he calls the 'I-and-Thou' dialogue. For Buber, this I-Thou relationship is the deepest and most meaningful encounter that is possible between two persons.

There are three ways we may communicate with other persons:

1) Trivial Chatter.

According to Buber, these kinds of superficial discussions — about, for example, soap operas, television in general, the world of worldly things — although very common, have little value.

2) The I-It Relationship.

In this exchange, we utilize the other person either to secure information ("What time is it? ... How much does that cost?"), to transact business, to dominate in some way, or to magnify our own importance or achievements. The "it" in the relationship could be any person, and since that person is interchangeable with any other, the person's essential uniqueness becomes unimportant.

3) The I-Thou Relationship.

When two persons engage in this I-Thou relationship, they are relating to each other with complete sincerity.

There is no trivia, no falsehood, no attempt to manipulate the other person. Both persons join, yet retain their unique individuality. Both persons feel something special about the conversation, and may be touched deeply, opened, and transformed.

Persons who have experienced these moments of I-Thou contact will always remember them. These memorable moments are more likely to happen when both persons are open, interested, and concentrating on the interaction. If we can't always reach the glorious heights of this I-Thou, then at the least we can listen to and talk with children with out utmost compassion and sincerity.

Responding To Problematic Behavior
with Interpersonal Techniques

The Opportunity-Problem below should be classified as an Interpersonal Problem. Solve it using one of the above Interpersonal Techniques.

Opportunity-Problem # 8. Kelly is Ostracized

In the playground, seven children are playing jumping rope games. Kelly, age 9, is sitting alone on a picnic table, looking as if she's just about to cry. The child-maintenance worker Audrey shouts to the jumping girls:

"Girls, why isn't Kelly playing with you?"

Three girls answer:

"Because she's weird."

"We don't want her to play."

"Because she can't jump."
The child-maintenance worker asks Kelly:
"Kelly, do you want to play with the other girls?"
Kelly nods her head, "Yes".

STOP and THINK

Don't jump to the solution! First, stop to think how you would manage this situation without using force or punishment. Write down your ideas, or discuss this situation with your spouse, relatives, co-workers, or friends. After you have thought thoroughly about it, you may proceed to the conclusion of this chapter. Solutions to all the Opportunity-Problems are given in Chapter 16.

Notes and Summary for Chapter 12

Parents, teachers, and all child-maintenance workers can use Interpersonal Techniques to heal relationships. Combined with Listening and Talking, these techniques can resolve problems quickly and effectively. Whenever we can help children to heal their broken interpersonal relationships, we solve immediate problems and prevent future ones.

Chapter 13

Technique # 9: The Time-In

Health at a very minimum is the ability to love, to work,
to play, and to think soundly.
— Ashley Montagu

The best way to manage misbehavior is to prevent it. A
'Time-In' is a time when adults and children play
together. Playing builds a rapport and friendship between
the grownups and the kids.

We shall soon see, in our essay about Neil Postman's
book (in Chapter 19), how the modern child has lost these
sacred secret worlds of play. To play for the sheer joy of
playing! That, firstly, is why play is so essential to
children: it gives them joy. Children who find joy in some
play that they love to do, will learn that life can be a
happy experience: there is no need for the life-wasters of
drugs, alcohol, or cigarettes. Play provides many other
necessary benefits. Play exercises the body. Play develops
the child's imagination and creativity. Through playing
together, children form healthy friendships with other
children and adults.

"Childhood is playhood," says A. S. Neill, the founder
and headmaster of Summerhill School.

In our modern culture, childhood is conspicuously devoid of spontaneous play. Parents and child-maintenance workers must give this world of play back to their children. There is no adequate substitute for this essential need.

There is much more that can be said about the theory of play than about the practice of it. Once the parent or child-maintenance worker appreciates the need for the child to play, then the next step is to play with the child, and encourage the child to play with other children.

Do children have more fun passively watching TV, or actively playing, either playing outdoors or playing imaginative games? ... Open the passive or disinterested child to the world of play, then watch the passiveness and the disinterest fade as the child re-discovers what he has been deprived of: a new joy in being alive.

When Not To Use and When To Use This Technique

In the moments when the child is harming (or about to harm) himself or others, then, obviously, we must intervene to stop the actions and prevent the harm.

For many other situations, the Time-In may be considered as the primary method to respond, or as a preventative measure, or as an excellent follow-up technique.

Responding To Problematic Behavior
By Giving the Child a Time-In

Use the ideas in this chapter to think about (and talk about, and write about) how to solve the difficult Opportunity-Problem below.

Opportunity-Problem # 9. Strong Mind, Weak Back

Albert, age 10, is so thin and so intellectual that he might accurately be described as "a brain on legs". Albert spends all day, every day, reading reading reading on his smartphone. Child-maintenance worker Larry is concerned that Albert is not interacting with other children, and not getting enough exercise. Larry asks Albert to play soccer with the other boys, but Albert refuses.

"You can't just read *all* day!" Larry says.

"By the time that John Stuart Mill was six years old," Larry replies, "he had read all of Plato's dialogues in the original Greek language."

Larry answers: "Take a break and play with the other kids just for a little while."

"No!" shouts Albert. "I don't want to!"

What should child-maintenance worker Larry say and do?

STOP and THINK

Don't jump to the solution! First, stop to think how you would manage this situation without using force or punishment. Write down your ideas, or discuss this situation with your spouse, relatives, co-workers, or friends. After you have thought thoroughly about it, you may proceed to the conclusion of this chapter.

Solutions to all the Opportunity-Problems are given in Chapter 16.

Notes and Summary for Chapter 13

Hermann Hesse has presciently written the motto of this chapter: "It is harder to kill something that is spiritually alive than it is to bring the dead back to life."

In today's screen-obsessed world, many kids have forgotten how to play. Instead, they have become passive watchers of meaningless television and computer games. The smart parent or child-maintenance worker can renew passive children by the technique of the Time-in, and by understanding the genuine needs of the child (see Chapter 23).

Every child needs Love and Friendship; Active and Imaginative Play; Contact with the Natural World; and experiences with Books and The Arts. The practice of weaning the child away from the slick screens toward life-giving activities is not difficult. It requires, for the most part, courage to try, and the enthusiasm to make it real.

♥

Chapter 14

Technique # 10:
Intervene Now! then L.E.N.D.
(Listen, Explain, Nourish, Design)

To those who are good I am good,
And to those who are not good I am good.
Thus, all get to be good.
— Lao Tzu

A violent world makes violent children.

And we are living in an extremely violent world. In the last decade, researchers reported that by the time the child has completed the sixth grade (in America that is approximately age 12), he has watched on television more than 8,000 murders and more than 100,000 acts of violence.

This violence in our media — and violence in our homes, schools, and sports — results in increased aggression in children of all ages.

Aggressive behavior, like all our other types of behavior problems, requires a non-punishing response from adults. Nevertheless, aggressive behavior is different, and more difficult to respond to, because it demands an intervention which is immediate.

Endangering Behavior (EB)

Endangering behavior (EB) is my term for moments when the child's behavior harms (or is about to harm) himself, another person, or another living being. The parent or CMW must act immediately to stop this behavior.

To intervene effectively, our response should consist of two parts:

First: Stop the problematic behavior.
Next: Find a way to help the aggressive child.

Our recommendation for responding to this variety of aggressive behavior is called the Technique of 'Intervene Now! then L. E. N. D.'

L. E. N. D. is an acronym:

Listen, Explain, Nourish, Design.

This chapter will explain this technique and how it can be used.

A Summary of the Technique of 'Intervene Now! then L. E. N. D.'

First, intervene and stop the problematic behavior; then Listen, Explain, Nourish with basic needs, and Design a plan to follow up and help the child.

Harmful behavior must be stopped immediately; then afterwards, to help the aggressive child, the parent or child-maintenance worker should listen, explain why harming others is not permitted, then nourish the child by giving him the opportunity to engage in the creative — not the destructive — activities of friendship, play, nature, books and the arts.

To make a complete commitment to the aggressive child, the parent or child-maintenance worker needs to design a plan which includes observing the child, intervening whenever needed, and continuing to nourish the child with the basic needs.

When Not To Use and When To Use
the Technique of 'Intervene Now! then L. E. N. D.'

When children are behaving without harming others or themselves, then we do not need to stop their actions immediately.

As stated above, there are two main types of situations when 'Intervene Now! then L. E. N. D.' is the technique of choice.

Firstly, use 'Intervene Now! then L. E. N. D.' whenever children are endangering their own health and safety, or the health and safety and others.

Secondly, this technique should be used to respond to aggressive actions: problematic behavior where one child (or more children) begin to fight.

Here are some examples of behaviors that require this technique:

- During a canoe trip, Harry is so wild that he rocks the boat.
- Jonathan, in a fit of anger, attempts to leave the school grounds, an act which would put himself in danger.
- Mary, quite contrary, is teasing a younger girl mercilessly, calling her nasty names.
- Zerp jumps on top of his friend Arnold and starts hitting Arnold, not in a playful way.

What About Harmful Speech?

Children should have the same rights as adults to free speech, except that they should not be permitted to use 'hate-speech' (words which denigrate a particular race or religion or gender), or 'harm-speech' (words which hurt the feelings of another person).

This last category, the words which hurt the feelings, must remain a judgement call by the parent or child-maintenance worker, since children often call their best friends the worst names. We cannot intervene every time one child calls another child a bonehead. A better plan is to teach each child that it doesn't matter if someone calls you a bonehead — what matters is that someone does not smack your head with a bone.

This Chapter 14 is concerned with actions (not mere words) which harm other persons. Words which are cruel can be handled effectively with the techniques discussed earlier in this book.

Rapport Is The Whole Key

Throughout this book we have talked about a number of terms and characteristics, many which appear again and again: calmness, sincerity, humor, listening, and replacing punishment with the balm of calm techniques. Possibly the most important of these — one which includes all on the previously-mentioned list — is the idea 'rapport'. The first task of every parent or child-maintenance worker is to establish a sincere rapport with each child. The parent or child-maintenance worker can accomplish this by listening to the child, by helping the child, by playing with the child, and by being thoroughly sincere.

In addition to the joy it gives to both the adult and the child, this friendly rapport has three remarkable results. Many problematic behaviors will be prevented. More difficult PBs will be able to be managed with relative ease. And problematic behavior which is impossible for some persons to resolve, will be possible for the parents or child-maintenance workers who have established this deep rapport.

What about Physical Restraint?

Parents and child-maintenance workers should use physical restraint as a last resort: if it is the only way to prevent the child from harming himself or harming another person. When this restraint is absolutely necessary, then always hold the child in a manner which does not harm the child.

The Technique of Intervene Now! then L. E. N. D.

How can a parent or child-maintenance worker apply the this technique?

Let's look at a brief example, step-by-step.

Step 1: Intervene Now!

Child-maintenance worker Robin is refereeing a soccer game, when one boy, Harry, explodes into a temper tantrum because he says he was pushed down just before the other team scored a goal. Robin sees that Harry is running toward Mark (the boy who pushed him), just about to tackle Mark and begin to fight. Child-maintenance worker Robin runs toward Harry, intending to hold him and prevent him from attacking Mark. Before Robin gets there, Harry's teammates have swarmed around him; they shout at him that if he fights, their team will get a penalty. The teammates hold Harry back from fighting Mark.

Step 2: Listen

With Harry beside him, child-maintenance worker Robin walks off the field and the soccer game resumes. Robin now listens deeply to Harry. Harry is angry, and swearing, but Robin doesn't care about this — Robin remains calm. After a few moments, Harry calms down.

Step 3: Explain

Robin explains that he saw the entire incident. Harry and Mark collided accidentally, and Mark also fell down at the same time. Child-maintenance worker Robin explained that this collision occurred far from the goal, and it did not effect the play in any way.

Step 4: Nourish

In this case, the nourishment is easy. Robin tells Harry that whenever he is calmed down, he can rejoin the game and continue playing.

Step 5: Design A Plan

Harry is easily upset by little things, much more so than the other boys, and whenever an interpersonal problem arises, Harry is more likely to fight than talk. Harry requires extra attention from Robin and from the other child-maintenance workers. Later in the day, Robin will inform his colleagues that he needs their help in watching Harry closely, and in responding to Harry calmly. Robin explains to his fellow child-maintenance workers that he has noticed that Harry is antagonized and angered even more when people who try to manage him are not calm. Robin will spend a few minutes every day reminding Harry that fighting is not the way to resolve problems: talking is the way. And every day Robin will increase his rapport with Harry, by sharing some activity together that they both enjoy.

Responding By Intervene Now! then L. E. N. D.

Review the ideas above, then try to solve this Opportunity-Problem with the technique of Intervene Now! then L. E. N. D.

Opportunity-Problem # 10. Sybil Disobedience

Sybil, age 9, needs less sleep than the other children. At 9:30 p.m. she walks out of her cabin. Her child-maintenance worker, Clare, is sitting outside on the picnic table. Clare's job this evening is to keep the girls in the cabins quiet, and to take any sick children to the nurse.

Clare: Sybil, please stop walking. It's too dark to walk tonight, there's no moon. I would like to walk with you, but I have to be here to watch the cabins in case any of the other girls need me tonight. Come over here and sit down with me, Sybil. We'll talk or play a game.

Sybil: No!

Sybil continues walking through the darkness.

Child-maintenance worker Clare walks, catches up to her, and talks to Sybil in a calm voice.

Clare: Sybil, you can walk back to the picnic table and sit with me, or I will carry you back. What do you want to do?

Sybil: Keep walking.

Sybil keeps walking.

Clare picks up Sybil and carries her back to the picnic table. Sybil screams, cries, and kicks her legs; and the noise wakes up twenty other girls.

Do you agree with Clare's response?

If yes, explain why you agree.

If no or maybe — you disagree or have some doubts — what would be some better ways to respond?

STOP and THINK

Don't jump to the solution! First, stop to think how you would manage this situation without using force or punishment. Write down your ideas, or discuss this situation with your spouse, relatives, co-workers, or friends. After you have thought thoroughly about it, you may proceed to the conclusion of this chapter. Solutions to all the Opportunity-Problems are given in Chapter 16.

Notes and Summary for Chapter 14

Which type of problematic behavior is the most difficult to manage?

Many persons will answer this way: the situations when we must act immediately to protect children from harming themselves or harming other persons.

Parents and child-maintenance workers need to stop this type of behavior immediately — but our response should not end then and there.

Parents and child-maintenance workers should try to heal the root causes of these problems, by Listening, by

Explaining, by Nourishing the Child with basic needs, and by Designing a plan to help this unique child.

To see dramatic examples about how this can be accomplished in practice, read the novel (published by Zorba Press) *Zen In The Art Of Child Maintenance.*

♥

Chapter 15

A Review and A Quick Chart
For Selecting The Best Techniques

This chapter reviews the 10 types of problematic behaviors which every parent and child-maintenance worker will encounter. In addition, this chapter reviews the 10 techniques that parents and child-maintenance workers can use to respond.

The **Quick Chart** in this chapter can be used as a guide to illustrate which techniques work best for each type of Problematic Behavior.

This chart is offered as a general guideline. Each situation with children is unique, and requires fresh thinking and a personal response. To enhance your educational journey, keep a diary or journal and make notes about which techniques you used, how you used them, what happened in each case, what you've learned, and what you might do differently the next time the situation arises.

The 10 Types Of Problematic Behavior (A through J)

A. Vitality Problems
B. Adultogenic Problems

C. Personal Problems

D. Respect Problems (Respect for the freedom and rights
    of other persons. Respect for other living beings.)

E. Safety and Health Problems

F. Motivation Problems

G. Money, Property, and Things Problems

H. Interpersonal Problems.

I. Passiveness-Listlessness Problems

J. Aggression Problems

Outline of the 10 Types of Techniques
For Responding to Problematic Behavior

1. Acceptance
2. Change the Circumstances
3. Listening and Talking
4. Teach the basic principle of 'Freedom, not License.'
5. Creative Role-Playing (CRP)
6. Motivation Techniques
    6.1 Share Your Enthusiasm
    6.2 Lead By Example
    6.3 Use Humor
    6.4 Make It Fun or Make It A Game
    6.5 Let Kids Participate in Making Decisions
        and Plans
    6.6 Offer Fun Alternatives (OFA)
    6.7 Ask Kids To Help Other Kids
    6.8 Give Nonmaterial Rewards
    6.9 Use Reason To Explain How/Why Your Goal
        is Worthwhile
    6.10 Discover and Remove The Root Of The Problem.

7. Pedocracy: the government by children
8. Interpersonal Techniques
    8.1. A.S.K. E.V.A.
    8.2 The 'We Technique'
    8.3 The Helping-Child
    8.4 The Technique of Good Deeds
    8.5 The Peacemaker
    8.6 The Finger of Fickle Fortune
    8.7 Repair By Rapport
    8.8 Listening and Talking
9. Give the Child a Time-In (Time For Playing Together)
10. Intervene Now! then L. E. N. D.
    10.1 Stop! the endangering behavior
    10.2 Listen
    10.3 Explain
    10.4 Nourish the Child by Providing Basic Needs
    10.5 Design a follow-up plan to help the child

How To Use the Quick Chart
To Select the Best Techniques

[The Quick Chart is on the last page of this chapter.]

    1. Find the Type of Problematic Behavior
(A to J, in the left column) that you need a solution for.
    2. Look down the column at the ratings: how effective each technique might be for this particular type of PB.
    The responses are rated this way:
- Excellent (**) is an Excellent technique for responding to this type of problem
- Good (*) is a Good technique for responding.

For example:

If Harry calls me "Noodlehead" then I would first try to understand what type of problem it is. Classified as a "Vitality problem" (Type 1), I would quickly realize that this problem requires my calm acceptance.

My response should be to

- Accept it, and smile, and ignore it; or
- Laugh at it; or
- Reply jokingly, á la: "My name is 'Michael Pasta', and Harry, I can call you, 'Harry canary'."

However, if the name that Harry calls me is extremely nasty — or if the name-calling is directed at another child — then this problem should be classified as an "Interpersonal Problem" (Type 8). And then I might use one of the Interpersonal Techniques — or I might just have a listen-and-talk with Harry.

Other ways to handle the situation (suggested by the chart, in the Good category) would be to use Creative Role-Playing (CRP) — so that Harry would understand how it feels to be called a 'noodlehead'; or to give Harry a Time-In, which would improve the rapport between Harry and the child-maintenance worker.

Quick Chart For Choosing The Best Techniques

On the chart on the next page:

2 stars means: Excellent way to respond **

1 star means: Good way to respond *

Quick Chart for Choosing the Best Techniques		
Problematic Behavior Type	* Good Technique	** Excellent Technique
A. Vitality Problems	1. Acceptance is the only way to respond.	1. Acceptance
B. Adultogenic Problems	3. Listening/Talking 7. Pedocracy	2. Change the Circumstances
C. Personal Problems	9. Time-In	3. Listening and Talking
D. Respect Problems	5. Role-Playing 7. Pedocracy 9. Time-In 10. Intervene Now!	3. Listening and Talking 4. Teach 'Freedom not License'
E. Safety and Health Problems	After intervening to keep kids healthy, use #s 3, 5, 9.	10. Intervene Now! then L.E.N.D.
F. Motivation Problems	2. Change Circumstances 5. CRP, 9. Time-In	6. Motivation Techniques 3. Listening/Talking
G. Money, Property, & Things Problems	5. Creative Role-Playing (CRP)	7. Pedocracy 3. Listening/Talking
H. Interpersonal Problems	5. Creative Role-Playing (CRP) 9. Time-In	8. Interpersonal Techniques 3. Listening/Talking
I. Passiveness-Listlessness Problems	2. Change Circumstances 3. Listening/Talking 5. CRP	9. Time-In
J. Aggression Problems	After 10. Intervene Now! — use #s 2, 3, 4, 5, 7, or 9.	10. Intervene Now! then L.E.N.D.

Chapter 16

Solutions
to the Opportunity-Problems

This chapter contains our solutions to the Opportunity-Problems numbers 1 through 10, in Chapters 5 through Chapter 14.

Remember that every Opportunity-Problem (O-P) has more than one good solution. And every good solution must be a response that does not use force, threats, rewards, or punishments.

Solution to the (Chapter 5)
Opportunity-Problem # 1. The Wisecracker

Type of P-B: Vitality Problems

Ideas and Strategy
A sense of humor, here and always, saves the day.
   It's essential to distinguish words from actions. Children must be free to say and to think what they want. Children must also learn that their actions must never harm another person.
   That is actions — but what about words?
   As children, we have often heard the chant:
      "Sticks and stones will break my bones
         but names can never hurt me."
   This is the ideal attitude for child-maintenance workers — to stay calm, and to never grow angry, when we are verbally disrespected or even insulted by a wisecracking child.

WHIRL (What Happened In Real Life)
   It's a mistake to be sarcastically cruel to a child, but perfectly fair to banter, and fight verbal fire with verbal fire.
   The child-maintenance worker smiled, pointed his finger at the child Toad, and then answered loudly:
   "Yes, it glows in the dark, almost as brightly as your head. Did your head get into a fight with a lawnmower and lose?"
   The 30 children standing there laughed wildly. The child-maintenance worker, still smiling, walked to Toad and then raised his hand for a high five. Toad slapped hands with the CMW. Soon after this scene they became friends.
      Note this well: the child-maintenance worker laughs when the wise-guy kid insults him. But if the wise-guy was being nasty to another child who is hurt by the stinging words, then it would be important for the CMW to intervene.

Solution to the (Chapter 6)
Opportunity-Problem # 2. A Homesick Runaway

Type of P-B: Personal Problems; Interpersonal Problems; and
Safety and Health Problems

Ideas and Strategy
The CMW has responded well. Now he should:
- Walk with Hubert, and continue talking with Hubert.
- Try to find out if Hubert's unhappiness is due to homesickness, or if it has a specific cause. A specific cause might be: another child threatened to beat him up; or the child is afraid of the woods, and so on. If there is a specific cause, talk with the child and ease his mind about that cause.
- Tell another CMW that he might need help with Hubert.

If words are unable to stop Hubert — or at least slow him down — and if Hubert is a manageable size, then say to Hubert:

"Hubert, you can walk back by yourself, or I am going to carry you back. What do you want to do?"

If Hubert is too big to hold, then walk with him.

Don't be shy about seeking help: Ask another CMW to bring the Director or supervisor.

WHIRL (What Happened In Real Life)
As CMW Herman walked with Hubert, they talked together, and Herman was able to discover the cause of the problem. That morning, Hubert had been yelled at by the sports coordinator. After walking for another five minutes, CMW Herman and Hubert sat down on a rock, and then talked. Soon after that talk, together they walked to the soccer field, to meet and talk with the sports coordinator.

Later that day, CMW Herman reported the situation to the youth program Director, who promptly yelled at the sports coordinator for his blunder of yelling at the child.

Solution to the (Chapter 7)
Opportunity-Problem # 3. Trouble at Home

Type of P-B: Personal Problems

Ideas and Strategy

When children bring the problems of home with them, there is often very little the CMW can do directly to cure the problem. What we can do is listen to the child, and help the child to make friendships. The home situation will remain the same, but the child himself will grow much stronger.

Note: If CMW Jim discovers that there is child abuse (or spouse abuse) — Jim should report these facts to his supervisor.

WHIRL (What Happened In Real Life)

CMW Jim sat down next to David. After lots more brooding, David told more of his story to Jim.

Jim: What exactly happens at home, David? You don't have to tell me if you don't want to.

David: Every day my Dad yells and screams at Mom for something stupid: dinner is late, or the shirts aren't ironed right, or the phone bill is too much money.

Jim: Does your dad ever hit your Mom?

David: He never hits her. Never.

Jim: Well, David, many dads have very difficult jobs, and it puts them under lots of stress. So when they get home, they yell at everybody. It's not your fault and it's not your Mom's fault.

Jim gave David a Time-in (see Chapter 13 in this book); later Jim found another CMW who had the same problem as David. The next day, Jim helped David to make friends with the other boys and girls in his group.

Though all this did not cure the root of the problem, it did give David more happiness and more self-esteem — which will help him to manage his feelings now, and in the future.

Solution to the (Chapter 8)
Opportunity-Problem # 4. Tattooing Trees

Type of P-B: Respect Problems

Ideas and Strategy
Yes, carving the tree is classified as misbehavior because it hurts a living thing. This type of misbehavior may be classified as type D, Respect problems. Because the misbehavior is done and cannot be undone, the CMW and the child should work together to find a solution — something they can do to make the situation better. And hopefully, make the child understand that it should never happen again.

WHIRL (What Happened In Real Life)
CMW Ben realized that he has made a mistake by speaking with the child in an angry tone of voice. So Ben continued talking, this time in a voice is calm, friendly, and sincere.

"Billy," said CMW Ben, "It's important not to hurt any living thing. The bark is the tree's skin. If you cut the bark, then insects and diseases could get in. The tree could die.

"And one more thing," said CMW Ben. "Instead of carving tree bark, there are many better ways to tell someone that you care about them."

Billy was silent for a long moment. Then he looked up and said: "Is the carving I just did going to kill the tree?"

The CMW answered: "Probably not. Let's read about damage to tree bark, and learn if there is anything we can do to heal it."

This became an STM (a Spontaneous Teachable Moment). Billy and CMW Ben searched the Internet.

"Look, Ben," said Billy. "The tree will survive as long as 75 percent of the bark is not hurt. It says to clean the wound, and do not add anything, but let the tree heal from the open air."

Solution to the (Chapter 9)
Opportunity-Problem # 5. Vanishing Kids

Type of P-B: Motivation Problems

Ideas and Strategy
A good rapport, between children and child-maintenance workers, prevents countless problematic behaviors. There are many solutions to this problem — the CMW found a good one.

WHIRL (What Happened In Real Life)
Unnoticed by the kids, the child-maintenance worker, Jeannette, watched the kids playing in the creek, then walked back to the cabin. One hour later, the kids returned.

Jeannette: How was drama, girls?

Girls: Great! Acting and pretending is so much fun!

Jeannette: You all deserve to win an Academy Award.

Girls: Jeanette, it's so hot today. Can we go to the pool and swim? It's not our day and time for swimming, but you can ask the Head Lifeguard to open the pool for us. Please, pretty please with maple syrup on top !

Jeanette: OK. I'm going to the pool now. You girls change into your bathing suits and meet me there in fifteen minutes.

Eager to go swimming, the girls changed, then ran to the pool. But where was Jeannette? The lifeguard told the girls that they can't go into the water until their child-maintenance worker gets there. The girls waited for thirty minutes. Then, one shrewd girl realized what was happening. When she told the other girls, they all ran to the creek.

They found Jeannette there, walking barefoot in the water.

"Girls," said Jeannette, "if you had told me that you wanted to skip drama and play in the creek, I would have let you."

The girls apologized, and then they hugged Jeannette.

Solution to the (Chapter 10)
Opportunity-Problem # 6. Slimy Teeth

Type of P-B: Motivation Problems

Ideas and Strategy
This is a genuine motivation problem because Melvin's teeth getting brushed is a worthwhile goal that needs to be done. With questions of health and safety there can be no compromise. The child-maintenance worker has tried to reason with Melvin, but reason failed.

Some children simply need reminders — many reminders. The CMW should have noticed, four days ago, that Melvin hasn't touched his brush. If his solution (below) had failed, then the next step would have been to explain to Melvin — without anger or threats — that the rules about health and safety cannot be broken.

In this situation, the "natural consequences" of Rudolf Dreikurs (see Chapter 24 in this book) cannot be applied — we cannot wait for Melvin to get the kind of agonizing toothaches that will teach him better oral hygiene.

WHIRL (What Happened In Real Life)
The CMW tried to explain more positive benefits of brushing your teeth. He told Melvin that brushing the teeth keeps your breath smelling fresh — and gives you a bright smile that makes you more attractive to girls.

After those positive ideas failed the inspire Melvin to use his toothbrush, the CMW solved the problem by using humor. The CMW made a monstrous face, grabbed Melvin, and screamed "Back! Back!". Playfully, he pulled Melvin into the cabin. Then the CMW brushed his own teeth as Melvin brushed Melvin's.

Solution to the (Chapter 11)
Opportunity-Problem # 7. A Broken Racket

Type of P-B: Money-Property-Things Problems

Ideas and Strategy

Here's another case where a problem with a material object could been anticipated.

As the kids say: "I would if I could but I can't so I won't."

If Dave had the money, he might volunteer to pay all or part of the total; but since he doesn't, he can't. Should he be punished because he's poor? Should he pay for a racket that broke with normal use? These are complex questions in the world of law. The other kids in the group thought the answers to both these questions were "no".

WHIRL (What Happened In Real Life)

The child-maintenance worker called all his kids together, including Dave and Mark, to discuss the issue. The children voted to ask the Director to replace Mark's tennis racket. The children also voted to contribute money so that they could buy Dave the basics that every other child had: a tennis racket; good sneakers; and a baseball glove.

Then the CMW brought Dave and Mark together, and asked them to talk together, and work out a solution that would be acceptable to both of them. Here is what they agreed on.

Mark: Dave, my Dad pays me to do different kinds of work for him, and maybe he can pay you, too. He pays the "living wage", which is now is fifteen dollars for one hour of work.

Dave: Fifteen bucks for one hour — wow! I'll work for that!

Mark: In less than 7 hours, you can pay me back, and then you can keep on working and keep the money for yourself.

Solution to the (Chapter 12)
Opportunity-Problem # 8. Kelly Is Ostracized

Type of P-B: Interpersonal Problems

Ideas and Strategy
Child-maintenance worker Audrey realizes that she can order the girls to let Kelly play, but she can't force the girls to be nice to Kelly — so it's not worth it to force the girls to let Kelly play.

The first solution to try would be to speak with each girl individually, one-to-one. To the three girls ostracizing Kelley, the CMW might say: "I am not happy when Kelly is miserable because the kids don't let her in the game. Think about this problem, and if you have any ideas about how to help me to solve it, tell me later tonight."

The smart CMW invites the children to participate in solving the problem.

WHIRL (What Happened In Real Life)
Albert Einstein wrote: "If you want your children to be intelligent, read them fairy tales. If you want them to be more intelligent, read them more fairy tales."

The CMW tried a unique solution. She gathered all the girls together — Kelly and the seven others — and she told them the famous story called "The Little Red Hen." Then Audrey said: "Until yesterday, this place was special because everyone was welcome in every activity, and everyone was treated as a friend. But yesterday I learned that everything changed, and that some people can be cut off from the fun. So if that's the way you like it, then I will do it, too. Today when I take the girls for special activities — swimming, and making pizza — I will not take everyone. I will take only the persons who I choose."

"That's not fair!" shouted the girls.

And then the next day they included Kelly in all their games.

Solution to the (Chapter 13)
Opportunity-Problem # 9. Strong Mind, Weak Back

Type of P-B: Passiveness-Listlessness Problems; Safety and
Health Problems; and Motivation Problems

Ideas and Strategy
- Encourage the kids to participate, but never force them.
- Teach by example.
- Speak with just the right words that the child will be able to understand and appreciate.
- Explain the natural benefits that the child will receive, when he changes his actions. For example, if he exercises, his concentration and memory will improve.
- Use a story or experience from your own life.

WHIRL (What Happened In Real Life)
CMW Larry decided that the first step to solving the problem was to establish a good rapport and friendship with Albert. So Larry talked about books, and he read stories to Albert and to the other boys. Larry and Albert wrote some stories together.

CMW Larry told Albert: "Plato was an athlete as well as a writer. During his college years, anthropologist Ashley Montagu practiced boxing. Chess world champion Magnus Carlsen loves to practice and play soccer. One of the best things that an artist or scholar can do for his mind is to house it in a healthy body."

After a few weeks, Larry discovered that Albert did not like to play soccer or other sports because he was so uncoordinated and unskillful compared to the other boys. Larry encouraged Albert to try individual and noncompetitive activities and games. Albert tried sprinting, to compare his time today with his time yesterday; and then Albert enjoyed jumping rope; playing catch; folk dancing; and shooting basketballs.

Solution to the (Chapter 14)
Opportunity-Problem # 10. Sybil Disobedience

Type of P-B: Safety and Health Problems

Ideas and Strategy
Much of our time working with children is spent having fun, playing outdoor games, and talking and listening. However there is another aspect to the work, and it is a serious one. Child-maintenance workers are responsible for the safety and health of the children. Whenever a safety problem or a health problem comes up, the child-maintenance worker must take action to keep the child healthy and safe.

Some of the work of keeping kids healthy and safe can be planned in advance, with sensible rules and guidelines. These rules should be made by the adults, and then carefully explained to the children, and then reviewed at regular intervals. Whenever CMWs explain rules to children, we should always explain the "whys" behind the rules.

But of course, the rules can't cover everything. Rumi has written: "Wherever you stand, be the soul of that place." Essential wisdom for child-maintenance workers caring for children is the practical interpretation of Rumi's words:

"Pay attention, think ahead, and be the one in charge."

WHIRL (What Happened In Real Life)
After Clare carried her back, Sybil kicked up a fuss for a few minutes; then Clare talked soothingly to her, calmed her down, then tucked her into bed. The next day, Clare talked with Sybil about the problem of waking up the other kids.

Bravo, Clare! Without getting angry, she did what needed to be done to protect Sybil. Sybil cannot be allowed to walk alone into the dark night, that would be too dangerous. From start to end, Clare has responded in the best possible way.

Part B

The Theory of Child Maintenance

Chapter 17

Childhood
Must Be Free From Violence —
The Genius of Alice Miller

"**F**ear and love cannot live together." — wrote the Stoic philosopher Seneca (4 BCE–65 CE). "Blows are used to correct brute beasts."
Two thousand years ago, the people of ancient Rome cheered enthusiastically as they watched gladiators fight each other to the death, and saw innocent persons torn to pieces by wild beasts. In that same era, Roman teachers practiced corporal punishment on a daily basis. The Roman schools were stocked with a variety of instruments used to beat children, including the ferula (a bundle of switches made from birch branches), the scutia (a whip made of leather straps), and the flagellum (a whip made of straps from ox-hide, the hardest available leather).

Although feeding slaves to lions and beating children in schools were acceptable practices to the mass of Roman citizens, occasionally a voice of protest cried out. The rhetorician Quintilian (BCE 35 to CE 95) wrote: "I am entirely against the practice of corporal punishment in education, although it is widespread ... In the first place it is disgusting and slavish treatment, which would certainly be regarded as an insult if it were not inflicted on boys. Further, the pupil whose mind is too coarse to be improved by censure will become as indifferent to blows as the worst of slaves. Finally, these chastisements would be entirely unnecessary if the teachers were patient and helpful."

After blaming teachers for failing to induce students to do what is right, and then asking how corporal punishers could possibly handle boys who cannot be influenced by fear, Quintilian adds: "And consider how shameful, how dangerous to modesty are the effects produced by the pain or fear of the victims. This feeling of shame cripples and unmans the spirit, making it flee from and detest the light of day."

Most Americans would condemn the Roman practices as backward, barbaric, and cruel. To me, it is remarkable that a similar savagery — the child abuse in our own homes and schools — is discussed so rarely, coldly, and superficially in American newspapers, television programs, and books. Our culture is poisoned by violence against children. In the year 2000, the US Department of Health and Human Services received 3 million reports of child maltreatment involving 5 million American children. Approximately 879,000 children (of the 5 million reported) were confirmed victims of child maltreatment, comprising neglect and medical neglect (63%), physical abuse (19%), sexual abuse (10%), and psychological maltreatment (8%). These numbers do not include the 400,000 children who were paddled that year — legally paddled — in American schools.

How can we explain the lack of private awareness and public action regarding the way we bruise and bully our beloved boys and girls? Where is the outrage from our authors and university professors who specialize in these fields? ... It appears to me that these thinkers have failed to understand the one most important thing: the essence of human nature. Like the church, too many writers have bellowed that children are inherently evil, and therefore — outside of heaven — there is little chance for individual fulfillment or social progress. This most dangerous myth — that babies are born with evil genes and children are by nature violent creatures — yielded a Nobel Prize for Literature to the author of that puerile fable, *Lord of The Flies.*

Fortunately, we can still find optimistic authors who believe that children are born good: Jean-Jacques Rousseau, Ralph Waldo Emerson, Walt Whitman, Pablo Casals, Helen Keller, A. S. Neill, Erich Fromm, Ashley Montagu, Abraham H. Maslow, Colin Wilson, Roberto Benigni, and the humble Michael Pastore. One more writer must be added to this prestigious list. Throughout the past twenty years, the psychiatrist Alice Miller has been the most passionate and articulate advocate for every child's natural goodness, and for each child's right to live free from violence. Miller's books include *For Your Own Good* (1983); *Thou Shalt Not Be Aware* (1985); *The Drama of the Gifted Child* (revised edition, 1996); *Banished Knowledge* (1997); and *Paths of Life* (1998). Miller's latest work — *The Truth Will Set You Free* (2001) — draws on the wisdom of the earlier volumes, but also introduces many new ideas.

Miller's argument, in *The Truth Will Set You Free*, might be summarized in this way:

1. Many adults manage their children with parenting and teaching methods which employ physical or emotional violence against the child.

2. Because of this violent treatment, the children grow up blind to the dangers of violent parenting, and out of touch with their true feelings and needs.

3. When these children grow to become teachers and parents, they will practice these same violent methods against their own children.

4. This cycle of "violence breeds more violence " can be broken, and abused adults can heal themselves and become nonviolent parents.

Miller begins by explaining, with many examples, how and why childhood reality is avoided "in six fields where we should expect precisely the opposite: medicine, psychotherapy, politics, the penal system, religion, and biography." ...

Miller's next section, 'How We Are Struck Emotionally Blind', offers an explanation for the remarkable and often-repeated story: "A father will beat his son and humiliate him with sarcastic remarks but not have any memory whatever of having been similarly humiliated by his own father." ... In the third part of the book, Miller offers examples of courageous adults who have healed themselves despite long histories of parental abuse.

Miller offers a stunning explanation about the mystery: "Why do people refuse to see and change their actions which are harmful to themselves and others?" ... In a previous book, *Paths Of Life* (1998), Miller says:

"People subjected to mistreatment in childhood may go on insisting all their lives that beatings are harmless and corporal punishment is salutary, although there is overwhelming, indeed conclusive, evidence to the contrary."

Written from the heart, this book explains the causes of our problems, and provides jargon-free solutions that work. Miller writes: "As a therapist I know that we can free ourselves from inherited patterns if we can find someone to believe us and stand by us, someone who instead of moralizing wants to help us live with the truth."

Along our road to individual freedom it is necessary for us to find what Miller calls an enlightened witness: a therapist, teacher, lawyer, or writer who is well-informed, open-minded, and willing to listen to the painful personal truths we need to tell.

In focusing on self-revelation as the key to freedom, Miller reminds me of the brilliant psychologist Sidney M. Jourard. In *The Transparent Self*, Jourard writes:

"We camouflage our true being before others to protect ourselves against criticism or rejection. This protection comes at a steep price. When we are not truly known by the other people in our lives, we are misunderstood. When we are misunderstood, especially by family and friends, we join the 'lonely crowd.' Worse, when we succeed in hiding our being from others, we tend to lose touch with our real selves. This loss of self contributes to illness in its myriad forms."

Only three years after the 1971 revised edition of *The Transparent Self* — Jourard died in an accident at age

48, too young to nurture his theory with the kind of real-life examples that make it more potent and therapeutic. Alice Miller has done this: filled her works with numerous examples of individuals who struggle and succeed in expressing their true selves in words and deeds. Miller's book is so honest about the lives of specific individuals, it reveals the inner life of us all.

The Truth Will Set You Free is Alice Miller's masterpiece, which shows us how we can face the darkest secrets of our painful childhoods, and emerge with hope, courage, and insights for living our lives more genuinely — more tenderly — with ourselves, and with the family and friends we care about. In my copy of the book I have marked scores of passages, passages that corroborate my intuitions and personal experiences working with children and adults of all ages and backgrounds. The book, with its stream of keen observations and profound ideas, moves us and enlightens us. "Trust men," writes R.W. Emerson, "and they will be true to you."

Inspired by Miller's book, I now understand much more clearly how to listen, and how to help other persons to free themselves by sharing the depths of their hearts and souls.

And there is one more essential lesson that this book may teach. Happy children with healthy childhoods are an endangered species. All of us involved in the helping professions must actively work to create a culture where violence against children, in all forms, is replaced with the three most valuable human gifts: reason, sincerity, and love.

Chapter 18

Four Scenes from the Film
The 400 Blows

================
The 400 Blows (1959)
a film directed by François Truffaut
In French, with English subtitles
94 minutes
================

Four Scenes from the Film The 400 Blows

(1) The Story

Antoine Doinel the film's protagonist —
aged 12 or 12-and-a-half — lives in a cramped
apartment in Paris with his selfish parents who
neglect him while his teachers punish him
too severely for a boy's playful misdeeds.

Where is the father? Where is the mother?
Despite his love of Balzac's *The Quest of the Absolute*
Antoine — unappreciated by pedantic instructors —
quits school then runs away from home
to live by his wits on the city's famous streets.

(2) The Puppet Show

A puppet show — the story of Red Riding Hood
in a theater packed with hundreds of young kids.
To warn the heroine the children scream and shout!
Young faces dance with fear then wonder then delight.
Young faces glow with pure sincerity and happiness.

Antoine and his only friend Rene sit half-watching
the performance as they talk about their new obsession —
getting money. Suddenly, we film-watchers grasp
 "Quel dommage! ... Their childhood died too soon!"
These boys are in more danger than Red Riding Hood.

(3) Stealing a Typewriter

Night. The boys tip-toe past the building guard
into the empty office of Antoine's father.
With no bag to conceal — and not realizing the machine
cannot be sold — they swipe a typewriter from Dad's
       desk.
(How unprepared they are for childhood and adulthood!)

Later, disguised by a hat only, Antoine tries to put it back
but the guard grabs him. His furious father drags him to
the police station. He spends the night locked in cages.
A few tears fall from his eyes as a police truck
drives him for a psychological evaluation at a
reform school — enthusiastically approved by his parents.

(4) Escape to the Sea

A short time at the new school is more than enough.
During a soccer game, Antoine runs to the field's edge
crawls under a wire fence and then dashes away.
He eludes the adult guardians chasing him
runs and runs until at last he arrives at the sea.

Seeing sand and sea for the first time!
A glimpse of eternity beyond innocence.
Dear boys, we escaped —now what shall we live for?
Love for Balzac and the movies gives Antoine
a slender yet hopeful chance to save himself
from the quiet desperation of his ordinary life.

— Michael Pastore

Chapter 19

Culture Against Childhood

G reat books, and their mind-opening ideas, can change your life. One of these that changed mine is Neil Postman's work *The Disappearance of Childhood*.

Why has this book moved me so profoundly? It corroborates what I had seen and grasped from my own experiences. It reveals the full breadth of the problem of modern childhood. And with great insight it explains the history and causes of childhood's rapid rise, flourish, and demise.

Postman's book was published originally in 1982; he added a short new preface in 1994, nine years before he died, in 2003. If we dare to read the daily newspaper headlines with both eyes open, it is clear in this Postmanic era the problems are just now being faced, and the crises have not passed.

In *The Disappearance Of Childhood*, Neil Postman calmly sets out to demonstrate a frightening idea: Electronic media — chiefly television — is eradicating childhood. This central thesis is explored via four original themes:

• Throughout most of history, there was no such thing as childhood as we know it;

• The invention of the printing press around 1450 led to literacy, schools, and the creation of modern childhood;

• Television is destroying that childhood; and

• Television both reflects and creates our culture which is filled with an incomplete personality type that Postman calls the 'adult-child,' too childish to be an adult, and too adulterated to be a child.

The book contains some interesting historical digressions, but for the most part the work explores these four themes.

Symptoms of The End of Childhood

What evidence exists to support Postman's theme that childhood isn't what it used to be? ... Fewer children are playing the way children played: actively, outdoors, without costly equipment, and free from interference by adults. Instead there has been a surge in organized sports for children: run by adults, financed by sponsors, and characterized by competition, rigorous training, and the fanatic desire to win. Postman points to other symptoms of vanishing childhood: children's clothing now resembles adult clothing; and the language children use and abuse — with its likes and you-knows and clichés and four-letter words — is hardly distinguishable from the language of poorly-educated adults.

Sexual activity in children (reflected by teenagers giving birth and getting STDs), has significantly increased. There has also been a marked rise in the number of children involved in the abuse of alcohol and drugs, along with a lowering of the ages of children who abuse these harmful substances.

Children are increasingly the victims of crime: more than 700,000 cases of child abuse were reported in 1980, and the estimated amount of total cases (reported and unreported) numbers more than 2 million. What can it mean that so many children are victims of crime perpetrated by adults? Postman argues this way: these facts demonstrate that adults no longer view children as children — as a special class of persons who require special protection and care.

More than any other variety of news stories, nothing seems to shake the nation more than the headlines and statistics about children committing serious crimes. The rate of adult crime — between 1950 and 1979 — increased 300 percent. During this 30-year time period, the rate of nonserious crimes committed by children — such as burglary, larceny, and auto theft — increased 8,300 percent.

What about children committing more serious crimes? Postman writes: "Between 1950 and 1979, the rate of serious crimes committed by children increased 11,000 percent!" Postman is a very calm, Socrates-like observer, and it is rare to find his prose punctuated with an exclamation point! Some things are shocking, even to the wise.

Childhood is a Recent Invention

In order to fully understand the present situation, we need to glance back at the past. For most of recorded history, there was no childhood as we know it. There was no social sense that children, up to age (say) seventeen, were different from adults; no understanding that children required special protection, nurturing, and education. Even as late as the year 1890, 93 percent of all American youth (ages 14-17) did not attend high school. Instead of schooling, these youth worked at adult jobs, often laboring more than 12 hours per day.

Before the 16th Century, children became adults at age 7, the age when they developed their full capacities for speech. In that pre-childhood era, children played the same games as adults, did the same work (as their abilities allowed), and shared the same culture. In terms of the law — which does not reflect justice but merely the way adults perceived children — children were treated as adults, and the same laws applied to all. Children who were convicted of stealing or murder could be — and were — mercilessly hanged.

The Printing Press, Reading, Schools, and Childhood

In the year 1453 everything began to change. Johann Gensfleisch Gutenberg tinkered with a winepress and transformed it into a printing press with movable type. The first wave of the information explosion illuminated Europe as Gutenberg's invention spread, and soon tens of thousands of books were speedily produced. And now reading mattered. To become a full-fledged adult, the child needed to do more than speak: she or he needed to learn to read. Thus, schools appeared, children were separated from the adult world, and childhood was gloriously born.

From approximately 1600 to 1950, the Western world refined and improved its concept of childhood. Children were assigned a special status. They were expected to behave, to play, to dress, and to learn as children, not as small adults. The world of the child was separate from the world of adults, and this unique child-world was acknowledged as essential for the healthy growth and development of the child.

How Television Precipitates The End Of Childhood

Everything changed again in 1950 with the proliferation of television. Childhood, which had thrived in the hundred years between 1850 and 1950, now begins its rapid and perilous decay. Postman acknowledges that there are other factors that contribute to childhood's end: the decline of the two-parent family, the increasing mobility and rootlessness of Americans, and — a theme of Paul Goodman in *Growing Up Absurd* — the absence of meaningful work by adults. But by far, the greatest contribution to childhood's plunge is our electronic media — radio, film, records, and especially TV.

How, exactly, does television accomplish the nefarious work of erasing childhood? To this question Postman offers three replies.

"Watching television requires no skills and develops no skills," he writes. Television delivers information in sound bites. (Postman had been talking about this concept before that term had actually been coined.) The average length of a TV sound bite is 3.5 seconds; for commercials it is reduced to 2.5 seconds.

Reading a book develops thinking and skills for analyzing, but sitting mesmerized in front of swiftly flickering images does nothing for the mind except diminish our attention spans. Whoever has watched a child concentrate with his whole self on a flower, an insect, or on any vital task will see this healthy state of mind contrasts radically with the zombified stupor which accompanies watching TV.

Television wounds childhood in another way: it is the same for everybody. Children are deprived of their special world as they watch the very same values, mores, and lifestyles that are watched by the adults. And let us not forget the commercials: by the time he reaches the age of 20, the average youth has viewed one million TV commercial ads.

Lastly, television eradicates childhood because it shows everything and it trivializes everything it shows. In the pre-television era, the adult and child world were separated. Then and there, children gradually learned the secrets, mysteries and horrors of the adult world at a pace they could safely manage.

Today, television throws everything instantly in their young faces: sex, violence, tragedy, greed, environmental catastrophes, incest, promiscuity, marital conflict, divorce, corruption, addiction, sadism, and more and more and more.

Do children need to be protected from all knowledge of violence and moral degeneration? ... No. But no child can remain a child and no childhood can remain a childhood if all this information comes too fast.

Bruno Bettelheim's book, *The Uses Of Enchantment*, explains how fairy tales allow children to understand evil without being traumatized. Unlike the fairy tales, television gives us no tools to comprehend, or to make peace with the horrors it conveys.

The Added Problem: The Adult-Child

There is one more fatal problem with TV. Although television ruins children by stealing their innocence and childlike qualities, it does not make them adults. The result of overexposure to television begets what Postman calls the "adult-child" hybrid. Adults who immerse themselves in TV become childish, self-centered, stuck in the present, desirous of immediate gratification, lacking foresight, and indifferent (like young children) to all consequences.

And children who share these television values become just like these immature adults: they lose their childhood and at the same time they never grow up. The behavior, attitudes, and physical appearance of children and adults are growing more and more alike, both moving toward this incomplete and unhappy creature called the adult-child.

Where Is The Wisdom We Have Lost In Knowledge?

Why is the current situation so devastating?

Postman answers:

" ... partly because I value the charm, curiosity, malleability, and innocence of childhood, and partly because I believe that human beings need first to be children before they can be grown-ups."

He believes that a society without literacy will revert back to the conditions which existed in the 15th Century, before the printing press. To borrow and bend from Thomas Hobbes: In those days the life of children was poor, nasty, brutish, solitary, unchildlike, and short.

Postman has accurately diagnosed the most serious malady of modern culture. Yet in this book, he refuses to prescribe: he will not come forth with answers and solutions about how we can save childhood and heal ourselves. Postman is more solution-focused in two later books, *The End of Education*, and *Building a Bridge to the 18th Century*.

What can we do about ths crisis in childhood?

We can establish new relationships with children, based in trust, freedom, and nonaggression.

George Eliot (the pen name of Mary Ann Evans) is one writer who has dared to show us — in her great novel, *Silas Marner* — a positive example of excellent child maintenance in action, based in a healthy love between a father and his child.

♥

Chapter 20

A Child Raised Without Punishment

My grandmother loved to read. One Sunday she came to visit, spit on her handkerchief, wiped it across my dirty face, and then gave me hundreds of her favorite books. For years, these beautifully-bound volumes gathered dust in our basement on tall wooden shelves. Patiently the books waited, unaffected by loneliness, as if they knew for certain that one day their time would come. And one day, when I had become a teenager searching for more from life than money and things, I dusted the shelves and discovered these magical books. As Henry Miller said when he made this discovery about the great books: "They were alive and they spoke to me."

There were complete sets of Shakespeare, Cervantes, and Dickens. There were mystery writers such as E. Phillips Oppenheim (1866-1946). Homer's *Iliad* and *Odyssey* sat proudly there, alongside *The Three Musketeers* (Athos, Porthos, Aramis, and D'artagnan) which made me wonder how writers could write if they could not even count. And there were countless classics, the books that people lined their bookshelves with but rarely read.

The first book which initiated my true love of reading was *The Yellow Crayon*, by Oppenheim. How much joy that story gave me! Soon afterwards I dived into Dickens's *Great Expectations*, and George Eliot's *Silas Marner*. There was not only joy here, but sadness, reality, insight, wisdom, foolishness, courage, struggle, hope — the whole iridescent spectrum of human feelings and experiences. In one moment I understood the value of literature: the great books illuminate reality, and teach us how to live with more freedom, more courage, more compassion, more authenticity, and more happiness.

In not-always-so merry England in the year 1861, the world was blessed with two remarkable novels about the effects of adults on children, and the power of children upon adults. The first of these is Charles Dickens's *Great Expectations*. Its evil protagonist, an abandoned spinster named Miss Havisham, adopts the beautiful young Estella, cultivates selfishness and cruelty in the child, then boasts: "I stole her heart away and put ice in its place."

The second novel, the subject of this chapter, is George Eliot's tender tale, *Silas Marner*. Silas had a promising future until age twenty-five, when he was unjustly accused of stealing money from a dying man. The real thief, his best friend, denounced him in front of the church-goers, then married Silas's fiancée. Disgraced, confused, and suffering from a complete loss of faith, Marner left his home then set up shop in the town of Ravenoe.

Silas Marner is a weaver who, for fifteen years in Ravenoe, has existed as a miser and a solitary man. Although not quite forty years old, Marner has condemned himself to a life of solitude. When neighboring boys peered through his window to watch him work, Silas would raise his head, then "his dreadful stare was always enough to make them take to their legs in terror."

Marner's workaholic days — almost sixteen hours every day including Sundays — are spent laboring at his spinning wheel. Every evening he ingested a meager meal, sat facing his fireplace, piled his beloved money into tall stacks, then gleefully counted his golden coins.

Most English novels end with a marriage and begin with a crime. Around Christmas Day, fifteen years after Marner arrived in Ravenoe, his isolated life — which had hit stone-bottom — plunges downward even more. Returning to his cottage one evening he opens up the hiding place under his floor, looks into the hole, and discovers that his holy gold is gone. The gold is gone! He searches the room thoroughly, realizes the tremendous fact that all his money has been stolen, then with trembling hands grasps his head and lets out "a wild ringing scream, the cry of desolation."

As a young man, poor Silas had been framed for robbery; fifteen years later he has been robbed of all his hoardings. At last, a cold and snowy New Year's Eve brings the third great event in Marner's life, the most significant of all. A young child, attracted by a flickering fire, toddles across the snow, enters Silas's cottage, then falls asleep beside the good warm hearth. Marner, with his failing eyesight, looks down and sees a golden glow. At first his heart leaps up and he believes it is his gold returned. And then he sees that the gold is the golden hair of a young child, one who reminds him of his infant sister who had perished when Silas was a boy.

Marner soon discovers that the child's mother has frozen to death in the snow. Despite offers of help from kind neighbors, he insists on keeping and raising the child, whom he names 'Eppie.' As he sits holding Eppie in his arms he feels a sacred awe, something akin to the mystic perception of William Blake's insight:

"Every thing that lives is holy."

Here is how author George Eliot describes the scene:

"She was perfectly quiet now, but not asleep — only soothed by sweet porridge and warmth into that wide-gazing calm which makes us older human beings, with our inward turmoil, feel a certain awe in the presence of a little child, such as we feel before some quiet majesty or beauty in the earth or sky — before a steady glowing planet, or a full-flowered eglantine [rose], or the bending trees over a silent pathway."

The time that the man and the child — father and adopted daughter — share together opens Silas to a genuine life of living and loving relationships.

"... as the weeks grew to months, the child created fresh and fresh links between his life and the lives from which he had hitherto shrunk continually into narrower isolation. Unlike the gold which needed nothing, and must be worshiped in close-locked solitude — which was hidden away from the daylight, was deaf to the song of birds, and started to no human tones — Eppie was a creature of endless claims and ever-growing desires, seeking and loving sunshine, and living sounds, and living movements; making trial of everything, with trust in new joy, and stirring the human kindness in all eyes that looked on her. The gold had kept his thoughts in an ever-repeated circle, leading to nothing beyond itself; but Eppie was an object compacted of changes and hopes that forced his thoughts onward, and carried them far away from their old eager pacing towards the same blank limit — carried them away to the new things that would come with the coming years, when Eppie would have learned to understand how her father Silas cared for her; and made him look for images of that time in the ties and charities that bound together the families of his neighbours. The gold had asked that he should sit weaving longer and longer, deafened and blinded more and more to all things except the monotony of his loom and the repetition of his web; but Eppie called him away from his weaving, and made him think all its pauses a holiday, reawakening his senses with her fresh life, even to the old winter-flies that came crawling forth in the early spring sunshine, and warming him into joy because she had joy."

At the age of three, Eppie "developed a fine capacity for mischief, and for devising ingenious ways of being troublesome." A well-meaning neighboring mother named Dolly Winthrop advised Silas "that punishment was good for Eppie, and that, as for rearing a child without making it tingle a little in soft and safe places now and then, it was not to be done."

Dolly Winthrop tells Silas that if he doesn't punish the girl, "she'll get so masterful, there'll be no holding her." As an alternative to smacking on the bottom, she suggests that Silas should shut her up in the coal-hole, a small closet near the hearth. Silas places Eppie there for a few seconds, then immediately lets her out again. One-half hour later he finds that Eppie is hiding in the coal-hole, laughing and enjoying the game. Eliot writes:

"This total failure of the coal-hole discipline shook Silas's belief in the efficacy of punishment. 'She'd take it all for fun,' he observed to Dolly, 'if I didn't hurt her, and that I can't do, Mrs. Winthrop. If she makes me a bit o' trouble, I can bear it. And she's got no tricks but what she'll grow out of.'

"'Well, that's partly true, Master Marner,' said Dolly, sympathetically; 'and if you can't bring your mind to frighten her off touching things, you must do what you can to keep 'em out of her way.' ... So Eppie was reared without punishment, the burden of her misdeeds being borne vicariously by father Silas. The stone hut was made a soft nest for her, lined with downy patience: and also in the world that lay beyond the stone hut she knew nothing of frowns and denials."

So Eppie was reared without punishment. And the father learned everything essential from the child. And now, children no longer scurried fearfully from Marner's once-terrifying glare.

"No child was afraid of approaching Silas when Eppie was near him: there was no repulsion around him now, either for young or old; for the little child had come to link him once more with the whole world. There was love between him and the child that blent them into one, and there was love between the child and the world — from men and women with parental looks and tones, to the red lady-birds and the round pebbles."

Sixteen years pass by.

The experiment in child-rearing without punishment has obviously succeeded, for Eppie has lived joyfully with her adopted father for all those years, and now she is eighteen years old, a young woman gentle, cheerful, and beautiful. Good fortune comes to the pair when Silas's stolen money is found and returned to him. And then a mixed blessing: Eppie's biological father reveals himself. He and his wife are wealthy, and they offer to take Eppie to live with them, and to give her all the luxuries and advantages that a young lady in society would require.

In the most touching of endings, Eppie refuses these offers then insists on remaining with her father Silas. "Eppie did not come forward and curtsy, as she had done before. She held Silas's hand in hers, and grasped it firmly — it was a weaver's hand, with a palm and finger-tips that were sensitive to such pressure — while she spoke with colder decision than before."

"'Thank you, ma'am — thank you, sir, for your offers — they're very great, and far above my wish. For I should have no delight i' life any more if I was forced to go away from my father, and knew he was sitting at home, a-thinking of me and feeling lone. We've been used to be happy together every day, and I can't think o' no happiness without him. And he says he'd nobody i' the world till I was sent to him, and he'd have nothing when I was gone. And he's took care of me and loved me from the first, and I'll cleave to him as long as he lives, and nobody shall ever come between him and me.'"

In *Silas Marner*, Eliot has shown us the goodness, and radiance of childhood, and a variety of deep relationships between children and adults which are both possible and priceless beyond gold.

Eliot's story took place in rural England around the year 1815, more than two hundred years ago. Since then, our cynical age has grown blind to the radiant qualities of the child. This narrowing of vision along with other social forces — the hectic pace of life, poor parenting techniques, television, Internet, neglect, miseducation, too much poverty, too much wealth, violence, consumerism — all have assailed children and sapped their radiant vitality. Our children are less innocent, less joyful, less childlike. Relationships between adults and children are often antagonistic and cold instead of cooperative and sincere.

How and why this has happened (how modern children and childhood became endangered) has been discussed in Chapter 19. How we can begin to heal this problem (by using nonviolent management techniques) is the theme of Part A of this book. Now we will examine an old-fashioned technology that always gives us fresh inspiration and new ideas.

♥

Chapter 21

The Problem of Violence and the Wisdom of Books

Technology can blow us up but never calm us down. Money can buy a piece of pie but not a peace of mind. Violence can stop one problem and then cause ten problems more.

Througout history, in all places and times, human beings have been haunted by the spectre of violence. One answer, simultaneously, is so far and so near.

Once upon a Time, writers believed that poetry and novels could do more than entertain us — they could also teach us, and enlighten us. Nathaniel Hawthorne, one of these idealistic writers, neck-deep in sin-hating Puritan New England, spent his literary career obsessed with exploring the problem of violence in the heart of men. In Hawthorne's 1844 tale *Earth's Holocaust,* all Earth's inhabitants (a mere 1 billion in those days) decided that the world had become so overburdened with useless junk, they should eradicate the trumpery by making one great bonfire and burning everything superfluous. The first things to be incinerated were yesterday's newspapers and magazines; then the robes and crowns of kings; then barrels of alcoholic beverages, until not a drop of drink could anywhere be found. The blaze rose skyward as people threw in every gun in the world, then every cannon, musket and sword. Then all the paper money fanned the flames; followed by [Trigger Warning for Bibliophiles: Start] all the world's books. [Trigger Warning for Bibliophiles: End] At last, the ferocious fire roared tremendously when it had been fueled with all the material symbols of religion: crosses and priestly garb.

Shorn of these obstacles to happiness — kings, weapons, information, money, and faith — all the people who had gathered round the fire expected a new world to appear. Yet one member of the spectating masses did not believe in external solutions. When this doubting stranger was asked what the world had forgotten to throw into the fire, he replied:

"What but the human heart itself?" said the dark-visaged stranger, with a portentous grin. "And unless they hit upon some method of purifying that foul cavern ... it will be the old world yet."

Let us believe and act on the belief that that cavern is not foul, and we can create the world anew. Laws can help us: We need humane laws to protect children from physical punishment, to educate the whole child, to save the Earths's environment, to equally share the world's resources, to eliminate weapons small and large. Compassionate actions can help us: Every adult should joyfully devote some time each week to improving his own neighborhood and town. Simplifying our lives and living what has been called the "sustainable lifestyle" can help us: we might work less, buy less, walk more, laugh more, spend less time in front of screens, and share more time with the natural world and with persons who we care about.

Most important is the motto "Begin with oneself," and the sublime Time-management advice: "Use your leisure time to cultivate your heart and mind." For this journey inward we will need honest guides — not to follow, never! since each of us is unique — to corroborate our self-discoveries. There are thousands of false prophets to sell you their folly for a fat price. Where can we turn to find genuine wisdom? ... A few solitary voices have been whispering:

"Look in the great books."

"Books?" whine the sophisticated critics, with a smear of scorn so thick, you would need a handkerchief to wipe it off their lips. "Humble, simple, old-fashioned, low-tech, freely-available books?"

Yes, books. I believe that in our best books we can find the psychological insights, the moral truths, and the emotional wisdom that we need to guide us through these difficult too-violent days. When books are written for the right reasons they contain the heart's treasures, the best that has been thought and said. Thoreau revered them:

"How many a man has dated a new era in his life from the reading of a book."

Aldous Huxley celebrated their beneficial effects:

"Every man who knows how to read has it in his power to magnify himself, to multiply the ways in which he exists, to make his life full, significant, and interesting."

These booklovers do not mean for us to pluck the plastic fruits from the bestseller lists, the volumes that Harold Bloom was talking about when he said: "I can hardly call them books at all." We rarely learn from the books written by writers who want to get rich quickly, since these books promote the god named Buynow, as they ignore the genuine sufferings and struggles of human hearts and human lives.

Leo Tolstoy envisioned the kind of Art and artists that we need. In his essay *What Is Art?*, he wrote:

"The artist of the future will understand that to compose a fairy tale, a little song which will touch, a lullaby or a riddle which will entertain, a jest which will amuse, or to draw a sketch such as will delight dozens of generations or millions of children and adults, is incomparably more important and more fruitful than to compose a novel, or a symphony, or paint a picture, of the kind which diverts some members of the wealthy classes for a short time and is then for ever forgotten. The region of this art of the simplest feelings accessible to all is enormous, and it is as yet almost untouched."

We need Tolstoy's pure simplicity. And more: in our complex and chaotic world, to make things clear for us, we need writers who know everything about everything essential. Michael Charles Tobias, in his 2021 memoir *The Earth in Fragments*, writes: "I want to believe that all of us even have time to read a few lines of verse, to take stock of our endless contexts, and to imagine better days …".

Most of us pay to read seductively-packaged garbage, ignoring the great books available for free. Can those old books in the library stacks help us — and help our children — to understand the problem of violence, and the problem of loving others and fulfilling ourselves? ... Some people laugh at this notion, and others swear that for two thousand years it has been true.

Many societies have been quicker to grasp the connection between stories and a healthy life. We marvel at the advanced civilization of the ancient Greeks, forgetting that these Greeks educated their children by asking every child to memorize Homer's epic poem, the *Odyssey*, a lively tome with 33,333 poetic lines. As Henry Miller remarked, we mistakenly assert that the Greeks humanized the gods: it was the gods — the stories about the gods — that humanized the Greeks.

Books alone cannot help us: not gulping down books like candy, ingesting them uncritically, the way we devour our junk food, films, and TV. What I am suggesting is more difficult. We can change ourselves positively, and help our children profoundly, if we learn these three rare arts: the art of reading deeply, the art of asking questions, and the art of talking sincerely with each other about essential questions, problems and ideas.

At this simple song of moderate optimism, I hear a humbug of cynics shouting "Preposterous! Absurd! Impossible!" ... Yet how many Americans can say that they have ever bothered to introduce themselves to the treasure-caves of Emerson, Thoreau, Whitman, Hawthorne, Melville, Emily Dickinson, and Louisa May Alcott?

We bend down to the pavement to pick up a dime, but we rarely reach up to the bookshelf to grasp the priceless treasures in our best books.

Many centuries ago a wise man said: "Do not depend on others. There is no grace, no help to be had from the outside."

Here, it seems to me, is the essence of the modern problem: some of us have given up hope altogether, while others of us are passively waiting, waiting to be rescued by new politics, new politicians, new prosperity, new inventions, or new laws.

There is an alternative between despair and passiveness. We can cultivate our gardens. We can educate ourselves by letting Nature, and Literature, and the Arts enter into and enrich our own lives. We can learn how to talk with our children by first listening to them, seeing them with new eyes, and trusting that we can learn from each child at least as much as we can teach.

The humbug of cynics, hearts frozen by the Snow Queen's ice, will always circle overhead and screech "Impractical, immutable, impossible!" And we who have found books filled with treasures —wisdom and new worlds and joy — will always be singing:

"No one knows how much she can accomplish until she tries."

♥

See Appendixes A, B, C, and D
for our four lists of great books and films
for children and adults.

Chapter 22

36 New Ways To Think About Kids

Before offering
sweets, or waving the mean stick —
Stop! ... I see this child !
— Hokkumeboshi, in *Zenlightenment*

Dear Reader: This chapter asks you to think about and then write about thirty-six essential ideas. They are written by women and men who believe that children thrive only when adults raise children in an atmosphere of freedom, creativity, and nonviolence.

The deeper we understand these ideas, the easier it will be to work with kids. When we understand the child's needs we can create happy children. Thus we will learn how to prevent some (or a great amount of !) problematic behavior, and how to respond in ways which heals the roots of the problematic behaviors which do arise.

The 36 ideas fall into 8 categories about essential aspects of working with children. Category "A" might at first seem strangely out of place — it is about self-realizaton, self-development, and self-improvement. The idea is that we need a healthy tree to make a healthy fruit.

How To Work with These 36 Ideas

A) Get a blank notebook and a pen.

B) Starting with idea number 1, write down your impressions of the idea, as if you were explaining what it means to you to a close friend.

C) After you have explained the idea, write down how a child might feel if an adult treated her with this idea in mind.

The 8 Categories of Ideas

A. How can we (adults) improve our own lives?
B. What are the qualities and traits of children?
C. How can adults establish a genuine rapport with each child?
D. What are some aspects of good teaching and learning?
E. Why do children misbehave?
F. What are some negative aspects and consequences of punishing children?
G. What is unconditional love? Why do children need it?
H. How can we, why should we, teach and help children instead of punishing and rewarding them?

A. How can we (adults) improve our own lives ?

A difficult question! ... To care for others we must first care for ourselves. Who we are — how happy, how tender, how honest, how wise — affects our children more than any other factor.

Ashley Montagu, the great anthropologist and author, states that human beings have been genetically designed to continue to learn and to grow throughout all the days of our lives.

1. I am still learning.
— Motto that Michelangelo placed over the door of his workshop when he reached the age of 70.

2. So much of our distress comes from the habit of regarding life as an enemy, and feeling it a duty to fight it, instead of seeing it as a friend, loving it, and agreeing with it.
— E. Graham Howe

3. You can only love a child if you become a child yourself.
— A. S. Neill

4. The meaning of life is to live as if life and love were one.
— Ashley Montagu

B. What are the qualities and traits of children?

We have heard from George Eliot (in her novel *Silas Marner*) that Nature blesses children with remarkable qualities, capacities, and potentials. To see these glorious qualities is the first step to learning how to bring them into being. The vitality of children is always in conflict with the dull routine of the adult workaday world.

5. Every child is an artist. The problem is how to remain an artist once he grows up.
— Pablo Picasso

6. Children think not of the past, nor what is to come, but enjoy the present time, which few of us do.
— Jean de La Bruyere

7. Children are remarkable for their intelligence and enthusiasm, for their curiosity, their intolerance of shams, the clarity and ruthlessness of their vision.
— Aldous Huxley

8. Childhood is the world of miracle and wonder; as if creation rose, bathed in light, out of the darkness, utterly new and fresh and astonishing. The end of childhood is when things cease to astonish us. When the world seems familiar, when one has got used to existence, one has become an adult.
— Eugene Ionesco

C. How can adults establish a genuine rapport with each child?

Those adults who are successful with children have one common characteristic: they have a sincere, natural, and playful rapport with each child. This rapport is the key to everything. As in William Blake's poem about the thief and the angel, both attempting to steal a peach — the rapport makes all the difference between failure and success.

9. The three most important rules for working with children are: Be sincere; Be sincere; and Be sincere.
—Michael Pastore

10. I do not teach children, I give them joy.
—Isadora Duncan

11. You can do anything with children if only you play with them.
—Otto von Bismarck

12. If a child is to keep alive his inborn sense of wonder, he needs the companionship of at least one adult who can share it, rediscovering with him the joy, excitement and mystery of the world we live in.
—Rachel Carson

D. What are some aspects of good teaching and learning?

How wonderful and rare it is to find a superb teacher in any field! She respects us, she shares her enthusiasms, she encourages us to ask questions, she learns with us as we learn.

13. Too often we give children answers to remember rather than problems to solve.
—Roger Lewin

14. Teaching by example is not the main way to teach. It is the only way.
—Albert Schweitzer

15. In the beginning he used to shake his head and wonder how it could be that the children understood everything that I said and almost nothing that he said; and then he laughed at me when I told him that neither of us could teach the children anything, but that they could teach us.
—Dostoyevsky, *The Idiot*

16. The future of mankind depends on the education of children.
—Aristotle

E. Why do children misbehave?

Throughout this book we have praised children, enumerated their splendid characteristics, and even hinted that adults can learn many important things from kids.

If children are so great, then, why do children misbehave? Not because they are born evil. Kids misbehave because they need something that we adults have failed to give.

17. I am malicious because I am miserable.
— Victor Frankenstein's monster, in *Frankenstein; or, The Modern Prometheus*, a novel by Mary Shelley

18. The difficult child is the child who is unhappy. He is at war with himself; and in consequence he is at war with the whole world.
—A. S. Neill

19. Destructiveness is the outcome of unlived lives.
—Erich Fromm

20. But a child only makes moral progress when he is happy. The true maxim runs that if we are happy we shall be good.
—Homer Lane, in *Talks to Parents and Teachers* (1928)

F. What are some negative aspects and consequences of punishing children?

Punishment is harmful to children, and punishment does not work. The more severe the punishment, the more harmful and less effective it turns out to be.

21. But punishment of children comes under the heading of adult interference with life itself. Facing the question frankly and openly we have to grant that most punishing stems from the irritation of adults simply because childhood is not young adulthood; children and grownups are in many ways antagonist in their interests.
— A. S. Neill (1883-1973), in *The Problem Child* (1926)

22. The fault no child every loses is the one he is punished for.
— Cesare Beccaria

23. A Russian Princess told Tolstoy's grandmother that (the Princess) believes it is necessary to act upon children through fear, and for that reason she beats the children. Tolstoy's grandmother replied:
"That is very nice, only please, tell me, what refined feelings can you after that expect of your children?"
— from *Childhood* (1852) by Leo Tolstoy (1828-1910)

24. Whenever a child lies you will always find a severe parent. A lie would have no sense unless the truth were felt to be dangerous.
— Alfred Adler

G. What is unconditional love?
Why do children need it?

We need to learn how to love our children, to love our entire family, without fear and without conditions, whether or not they choose to follow our wishes or obey our commands. Having had love withheld from us, we withhold love from others. When we truly love someone we trust them, we have faith in them, and we give them as much freedom as they can manage, knowing that this freedom is necessary for their optimum growth.

25. Love yields in one moment what years of effort can hardly attain.
— Goethe

26. Children need love, especially when they do not deserve it.
— H. S. Hulbert

27. Love is the child of freedom,
    never that of domination.
— Erich Fromm

28. To those who are sincere to me I am sincere
    and to those who are not sincere I am sincere.
    And thus all get to be sincere.
— Lao Tzu

H. Instead of punishing and rewarding: How can we, and why should we, teach and help children ?

Adults need to become teachers and helpers to children, not bribers and punishers.

When your best friend shows up late for your hike in the park, do you shout at him and send him to his room?

Of course not.

Yet, every day, adults treat their children with less respect than they give to their neighbors and friends. Punishment is outmoded. It is time to find wiser, kinder, more creative ways.

29. If a child tells a lie, tell him that he has told a lie, but don't call him a liar. If you define him as a liar, you break down his confidence in his own character.
— Jean Paul Richter, pseudonym, Jean Paul (1763—1825)

30. Children have never been very good at listening to their elders, but they have never failed to imitate them.
— James Baldwin

31. Power is like holding an egg in your hand. If you hold too tightly, you crush the egg; if you hold too loosely, you drop the egg and it breaks.
— African proverb

32. The truth must be spoken lovingly.
— Henry David Thoreau

33. A human being should always respond,
   but never react.
— Ashley Montagu

34. If you want to help people, don't get angry with them.
— Kalahari bushman

35. What is power? ... Power is the ability to understand and apply alternatives in a given situation.
— Author unknown; heard and noted at a lecture about conflict resolution and Taoism.

36. If there is anything we wish to change in the child, we should first examine it and see whether it is not something that could better be changed in ourselves.
— Carl Gustav Jung, *The Development of Personality*

> Laugh, be optimistic, be happy.
> Play and have fun together.
> Give children the three greatest gifts:
> sincerity, compassion, and joy.
>
> — Michael Pastore

Each second we live is a new and unique moment of the universe, a moment that will never be again And what do we teach our children? We teach them that two and two make four, and that Paris is the capital of France. When will we also teach them what they are? We should say to each of them: Do you know what you are? You are a marvel. You are unique. In all the years that have passed, there has never been another child like you. Your legs, your arms, your clever fingers, the way you move. You may become a Shakespeare, a Michaelangelo, a Beethoven. You have the capacity for anything. Yes, you are a marvel. And when you grow up, can you then harm another who is, like you, a marvel? You must work, we must all work, to make the world worthy of its children.

— Pablo Casals

Chapter 23

Enlightened Education for Happy Children

Enlightened Education. The term has a soothing, avant-garde, inspiring ring to it — but what does it mean?

All children have basic needs. In addition to an environment that allows the child to be safe and physically healthy, the eight most important needs of children are:

1. The need to Love and to be loved.
2. The need for active Play.
3. The need for Freedom to develop in their own way.
4. The need for Sincerity and integrity from adults and the adult world.
5. The need for an appreciation of Nature, the outdoors, and living beings.
6. The need for Sustainable Living, a lifestyle where humans live in harmony with the land and all living beings, in "simplicity, beauty, and permanence".
7. The need for practicing Creative Activities and the Arts.
8. The need for Stories that Educate the Imagination.

Whenever these needs are fulfilled, the child will grow into a happy and healthy human being. Whenever these needs are denied, the child will develop neuroses, become unhappy, and harm himself or other living beings.

There is one more need that is more complex, one that might be called "emotional security." Children in the 21st Century must endure an epidemic of violence, and — perhaps even more dangerous — the fear that a world permeated by violence brings. Fear is the greatest obstacle to self-fulfillment, to living life creatively, freely, joyfully.

A. S. Neill, the founder of Summerhill School, has written:

"A child most certainly acquires fears from the world around him. Today, even small children cannot help hearing about coming wars with their terrible atom bombs. It is only natural to associate fear with such things. But if there is no unconscious fear of sex and hell to compound the reality-fear of bombs, the fear of bombs will be a normal one — not a phobia, not a pervasive anxiety. Healthy, free children do not fear the future. They anticipate it gladly. Their children in their turn will face life without the sick fear of tomorrow."

Excessive fear has another powerful effect on children: it forces the child's inner world into a conflict with the external reality, by robbing the child of his optimistic vision of the world. "A child starts life with faith in goodness, love, justice," writes Erich Fromm, in The Heart of Man. But at some point in his life, a child experiences 'the shattering of faith' which leads to the hatred of life.

Rightly it has been said: "Youth ends when disillusionment begins."

How can we help a child to understand why his world is surrounded by violence? How can we help a child to replace her fears with courage, nonviolent actions, and faith in the goodness and potentialities of Life?

Enlightened Education is the answer. In homes and schools and summer camps, we need a new approach to child maintenance and education. This revolutionary education — grounded in freedom, in nonviolence, in noncommercialism, and in creativity — would revolve around the eight essential needs of the child.

This chapter briefly discusses how to meet six of the eight essential needs: Sincerity, the Arts, Books, and Love, and an Appreciation of Nature and Sustainable Living.

Sincerity

Adults and children need to share more time playing together, learning together, and talking together. When children ask questions, they should be answered with complete sincerity. In the novel *The Idiot*, Dostoyevsky's hero Prince Myshkin explains:

"I used to tell them everything, I concealed nothing from them ... Children can be told anything — anything. I've always been amazed by seeing how little grown-up people understand children, how little parents even understand their own children. Nothing should be concealed from children on the pretext that they are too little and that they are too young to understand. What an unfortunate idea!"

Telling a lie to a child is a grave mistake, because it hinders the intellectual and emotional development of the child. In Summerhill, A Radical Approach To Child Rearing, A. S. Neill states that in 38 years he never consciously told a lie to any of his pupils. Mr. Neill advises that adults should never lie to a child (except when a life could be saved by the lie), and then writes:

"There is no other way but the way of absolute truth for a child ... Lying is always cowardice, and cowardice is the result of ignorance."

How, then, might we answer a child who asks:

"Why is there so much violence in the world?"

And how to answer another common child's question, always asked with anxiousness:

"Why are there bad people in the world?"

We must answer with sincerity. We understand Fromm's insight, that "Destructiveness is the outcome of unlived lives."

Translating that same idea into a simpler language, we could say: "When persons are very unhappy, they may harm themselves or other persons."

And how should we respond to these unhappy persons? ... As we protect ourselves and others from harmful actions, we must always respect the person despite his misguided deeds.

Arts

The psychologist E. Graham Howe has written that there are four things that can heal us: Time, Sleep, Change, and Love. To that list I would add six more healing forces: walking, peak experiences, sincere conversations, contact with Nature, carefully reading good books, and practicing any of the Arts.

When I say 'the Arts' I do not mean staring at pictures on a museum wall: that can give us pleasure, but not the deep healing effects. Creating art — drawing, painting, singing, dancing, playing instruments, working with wood or clay — are the activities that can help us. Art in general can heal us, and the Art of Literature can help us to understand how to respond to violence. Even more significantly, children and adults who create are far less likely to commit violent acts.

The most powerful force on Earth is human energy. Our world is driven not only by flowing electrons, but also by passions, mind, and will. Our inner energies emerge in two types of actions: either life-harming — where the person hurts himself or others; or life-enhancing — where the person uses his vast energy for creativity in living, or creativity in making art.

Leo Tolstoy, Erich Fromm, and Herbert Read all have observed that there is a profound relationship between art and violence. How Art works to heal us and to transform us has been insightfully explained in Read's essay titled: *Art and Life*. Read writes:

"I am concerned with the social problem, with the anxiety, the all-prevailing sense of insecurity which undoubtedly motivates the crime and violence of our age. ... Unused energies, deprived of traditional outlets, explode in violence."

For Plato, and for Tolstoy, art is far more than an ornament, a luxury, a distraction, a pleasure, a solace, a trivial amusement. Commercial art — artificial, superficial, and mass-produced from formulas — has little power to effect us. But about genuine Art, Herbert Read explains, in that same essay that art has "the unique function of uniting men in love of each other and of life itself." In his masterpiece Education Through Art, Herbert Read proposes that the essence of the child's education should be comprised of two activities: Art and Play.

William Hughes Mearns (1875–1965) is another significant educator who writes about the importance of creativity and the arts in the lives of children. His two books on this theme are Creative Youth (1925), and Creative Power (1929).

Books

We have rarely dared to imagine the glorious immensity of human potential.

"Every child is an artist," said Picasso. "The problem is how to remain an artist once he grows up."

The foundation of all creativity is our imagination. Children have vivid imaginations; and the job of parents and teachers is to nurture these imaginations, and encourage their development. How? ... We do not need a complex answer when a simple one is so effective. To educate the child's imagination, inspire the child to love, to read, and to reflect about great stories and books.

Books help us to see other worlds, to see other minds, and to be tolerant of other values. The proper study of books can teach us empathy, literally "feeling in", so that we learn compassion for persons and living beings. Readers who identify with fictional characters can gain self-knowledge, self-forgiveness, and courage to face obstacles in their own lives.

Yet, as Thoreau stated, we have not yet learned to read deeply. Our education has ignored the imagination and focused instead on information, knowledge, and "the one thing needful" — facts. If American schools are failing, it may be because they have forgotten the needs of the whole child, and instead focused on the narrow task of imparting knowledge.

Too often, teachers and educational institutions are obsessed with cramming square information into round minds. The problem has plagued us for a long time. In 1854 Charles Dickens wrote a novel called Hard Times (subtitled For These Times), which describes public education at its worst. Students are mere numbers, human beings are slaves to their work and their machines, and learning is not only laborious but thoroughly disconnected with the realities of life. In the novel's opening scene, in "a plain, bare, monotonous vault of a schoolroom," schoolmaster Gradgrind bullies his subordinate teacher with his outmoded philosophy of instruction.

"Now, what I want is, Facts. Teach these boys and girls nothing but Facts. Facts alone are wanted in life.

Plant nothing else, and root out everything else. You can only form the minds of reasoning animals upon Facts: nothing else will ever be of service to them. This is the principle on which I bring up my own children, and this is the principle on which I bring up these children. Stick to the Facts, sir!"

Literature can have profound effects on children. An exceptionally eloquent advocate for the value of reading is the late Bruno Bettelheim. In his book, The Uses Of Enchantment: The Meaning and Importance of Fairy Tales, Bettelheim stated that fairy tales teach the child: "that a struggle against severe difficulties in life is unavoidable, is an intrinsic part of human existence — but that if one does not shy away, but steadfastedly meets unexpected and often unjust hardships, one masters all obstacles and at the end emerges victorious."

Another passionate advocate for reading is the author Barry Sanders. His illuminating book A Is For Ox: The Collapse of Literacy and the Rise of Violence in an Electronic Age, explained the reasons behind the new epidemic of youth violence. American children, who do not read worthwhile literature, have not developed the power of self-reflection, and therefore they can only lash out with aggressive acts. Sanders concludes that we should gather into small groups to discuss the most important issues of our times, with special concern for future generations.

Books and Ideas can be used to educate the child's imagination, and to give the child emotional security and inner strength.

Love

What do we mean by love? In The Art Of Loving, Erich Fromm explains the meaning of the theory and practice of this kind of relationship. For Fromm, love is not a feeling, not something you fall into, not something you hope will happen to you as you wait for the 'right' person. Love is an art which is practiced every day, an activity that requires giving the essence of your entire self.

I believe that healthy love contains three elements. The first element is caring for the other person. Love is understanding what the person needs then helping them to secure these needs.

The second element is relating to the other person in freedom. In healthy love, we never dominate (or submit to) the other persons; instead we treat the other persons with an equality and respect which allows each individual to be free to unfold his or her genuine self.

And thirdly: the act of love involves a deep joy in being together. Every relationship flourishes because of the joy we give and we receive in the presence of our family and friends.

Of course, all modern parents love their children. The real question is this: "How can adults learn to love children in a new and deeper manner, a way which helps each child to grow as a caring and creative human being?"

Love is incompatible with the use of force, threats, and punishments to control the child's behavior. In her book The Education of Children, Ellen Key writes:

"War, hunting for pleasure, corporal discipline, are nothing more than different expressions of the tiger nature still alive in man. When the rod is thrown away, and when, as someone has said, children are no longer boxed on their ears but are given magnifying glasses and photographic cameras to increase their capacity for life and for loving it, instead of learning to destroy it, real education in humanity will begin."

Love — blended with knowledge, insight and wisdom — is one thousand times more nurturing than the blind love or the selfish love that ignores the child's deepest needs.

Nature Appreciation and Sustainable Living

I propose this new international law:

Every child, in every nation must spend two weeks every year in a natural place, such as a state park or a summer camp.

If laws in the USA demand that children must spend 180 days every year sitting in classrooms in schools, then why not a mere 14 days living in the heart of nature ?

Here we would learn Nature appreciation, and the art of natural and sustainable living.

What is a Sustainable Society?

Acording to G. Tyler Miller:

A sustainable society is "a society based on working with nature by recycling and reusing discarded matter, by preventing pollution, by not unnecessarily wasting matter and energy resources, by preserving biodiversity, and by not allowing population size to exceed the carrying capacity of the environment."

Activities and Lessons for
Loving Nature and Sustainable Living

Here is a checklist for supervising adults who want to bring Nature into the lives of children.

1. Sleep Outdoors.
Are children in your program encouraged — and never forced — to sleep outdoors, at least once during their stay at camp?

2. Practice Recycling and Composting.
Many cities now require recycling, and encourage home composting. Kids can measure how much you compost.

3. Reduce Waste at the Source.
Buying in bulk saves loads of money, and greatly reduces the amount of waste generated from packaging materials.

4. Use the Right Amount of Food.
With good examples and interesting lessons, the amount of food thrown away after every meal can be enormously reduced.

5. Offer A Viable Vegan/Vegetarian Meal Option.
As the sage said: "If the main course is spaghetti and meatballs, then the vegan/vegetarian option should be more than just spaghetti." ... Understand — and discuss — the many important benefits that veganism/

vegetarianism brings to the health of the individual, and to the ecological health of the world.

6. Grow Some of your Food.
Gardening is an activity that is enjoyable, saves money, and brings you the healthiest possible foods.

7. Conserve Water.
By monitoring how much water used, and how long your showers are, you can learn to use much less.

8. Respect Everyone's Right to an Environment that is Noise-free.
Does the blasting of radio Muzak obscure the sounds of the natural world? ... Explain the need for everyone's right not to be polluted by unwanted noise.

9. Just Don't Smoke.
Is smoking prohibited on your grounds, and does someone explain to children the deadly effects of smoking? ... During discussions, emphasize the positive aspects of non-smoking, as well as the negative, such as: Non-smokers are healthier, and more attractive to other persons.

10. Know How Much Energy You Use.
Find out how much energy is being used, and plan ways to use less. Take extra credit for all energy that comes from renewable sources: sun, wind, hydrogen fuel cells.

11. No Punishments and No Rewards.
Adults who work with children are trained in nonviolent methods for managing children's problematic behavior.

12. Make it, Don't Buy It.
Repair old items instead of throwing them away.
Encourage the idea that many things we usually buy can
be made: from clothing to computers.

13. Fun is Free.
In Aldous Huxley's dystopian novel, *Brave New World*,
the human population has been brainwashed to believe
that to have fun requires a large amount of money and
the latest high-priced gear. Teach children to enjoy life
with creative activities: making music, poetry, art, and
dance.

14. Play For the Sheer Joy of Playing.
Offer cooperative games as an option to traditional
"winning means everything" sports. When competitive
sports are played, play them in the spirit of good
sportsmanship. Play not to win, play for the joy of the
game.

15. Move Thyself.
Encourage children to walk more, hike more, and ride
bicycles safely. Discourage sedentary activities that have
little or no personal or social value: i.e., excessive
watching television, or compulsive playing video games.

16.Teach Kids About Sustainable Living.
Give talks, and lead discussions, about earth-friendly
values and practices. First, of course, educate yourself.

17. Confront the Problem of Violent Video Games.
These games are now proven to be harmful to children.
Decide how you should manage this situation.

18. Encourage Reading, and Discussing Ideas in quality books.
Every child should know the works of the great authors and artists of her/his own nation, and the nations of the world.

19. Give Children a Voice and a Vote about decisions that matter to them.
Adults should decide about all health and safety issues, and children may be given a voice about everything else.

20. Teach "Respect All Living Beings."
Albert Schweitzer's theme "Reverence for Life," should be one of the essential underlying principles of every summer camp that aspires to be green, sustainable, and ecologicially healthy.

Sincerity, the Arts, Books, Love, Nature appreciation, and Sustainable Living.

This is the education for the present and for the future, that we can and must begin today: Enlightened Education.

♥

Chapter 24

Key Ideas in Child Maintenance

Understand and practice these terms and ideas, and they will help you to avoid mistakes, and to discover effective responses — to all varieties of children's behavior — that are calm, caring, and creative.

ABC Rule. ABC stands for Always Be Calm.

Adultogenic problems. Children's behavior problems that are caused by adults: by unnecessary restrictions, by rules not in the best interests of the child, or by harsh punishments.

Affirmation Cycle, the Positive (PAC). The Positive Affirmation Cycle is the way that relationships between adults and children grow deeper and friendlier. Grownups who want to deepen the relationship must respect the child, play with the child, listen to the child, give the child freedom. See, in this Chapter, Needs of children.

Aggravation Cycle, the Mutual (MAC). The Mutual Aggravation Cycle is the way that relationships between adults and children disintegrate. The child misbehaves, which prompts the grownup to act mean and strict, which makes the child frustrated and behave worse, which makes the grownup stricter and meaner, which makes the child behave worse — and so on and so on.

Anonymous Authority. This is Erich Fromm's idea, (see his book *Escape From Freedom*), explained succinctly in his foreword to A. S. Neill's book *Summerhill: A Radical Approach to Child Rearing*. "Overt authority is exercised directly and explicitly. The person in authority frankly tells the one who is subject to him, 'You must do this. If you do not, certain sanctions will be applied against you.' Anonymous authority tends to hide that force is being used. Anonymous authority pretends that there is no authority, that all is done with the consent of the individual. While the teacher of the past said to Johnny, 'You must do this. If you don't, I'll punish you.'; today's teacher says, 'I'm sure you'll like to do this.' Here, the sanction for disobedience is not corporal punishment, but the suffering face of the parent, or what is worse, conveying the feeling of not being 'adjusted,' of not acting as the crowd acts. Overt authority used physical force; anonymous authority employs psychic manipulation."

APT: the Axiom of Positive Teaching. It is better to teach what to do, than to tell the child what not to do.

Caring grownup. Any grownup who responds nonaggressively, instead of reacting unthinkingly, to children's misbehavior. *See* Robot grownup.

Caring response. Throughout this book you have been asked to give up the Way of Force — punishing, threatening, and yelling — and to replace these with words and actions that help the child. A caring response is any nonaggressive response, actions or words, which resolves or eases the misbehavior, and deepens the rapport between the adult and the child.

Child maintenance is the art, and the joyful work, of keeping a child in optimum physical and psychological health: giving the child the physical and emotional nourishment that s/he needs so that s/he will be able to love, to learn, to play, to appreciate Nature, to create, and to think soundly.

Child maintenance, Essential goals of. The essence of Child Maintenance is a three-part strategy for working with all types of children. The adult attempts to:

1) Prevent misbehavior: by listening, by respecting children (by not yelling, not threatening, etc.), and by teaching children the meaning of 'Freedom, not license'.
2) Respond whenever children misbehave, respond with words and actions that are calm, creative, and kind.
3) Nourish children by giving children what they need to enjoy a safe and happy childhood.

Child-maintenance worker (abbreviated CMW) is anyone who works with kids: a parent, a teacher, a counselor, a camp counselor or camp staff member, a childcare worker, a grandparent, a nanny, and more.

CMW. A child-maintenance worker (*See above*).

Creative Role-Playing (CRP) is an activity similar to improvisational drama: the players assume roles and act spontaneously, saying and doing whatever they think and feel. Conducted by a skilled leader, CRP becomes a powerful tool for teaching empathy ('feeling-in') and insight ('seeing-in') — to help us to imagine the heart and the mind of another human being.

Do-it-or-else! Method of child control is also called, the Way of Force. This barbaric and uncreative method may be summarized in one cold sentence: "Tell the child what to do; if he disobeys you, then threaten and punish him." The use of force — punishment, threats, intimidation, anger — is a foolish, boorish, and lose-lose attempt to control a child's behavior.

Endangering behavior (EB) is my term for moments when the child's behavior harms (or is about to harm) himself, another person, or another living being. The parent or CMW must act immediately to stop this behavior.

Force, the Way of. This is the use of force — punishment, threats, intimidation, anger — to attempt to control children's behavior. This barbaric and uncreative method may be summarized in one cold sentence: "Tell the child what to do; if he disobeys you, then threaten and punish him."

Freedom, not license. This is a basic principle of human relations, formulated by A.S. Neill and practiced in his school named Summerhill. Concisely stated: "Children should be given freedom to do what they like, but no one is allowed to hurt others, or to restrict another person's freedom." This abuse of freedom is called license. Erich Fromm, in his foreword to A.S. Neill's book *Summerhill*, explains it this way: "Freedom does not mean license. This very important principle, emphasized by Neill, is that respect for the individual must be mutual. A teacher does not use force against a child, nor has a child the right to use force against a teacher. A child may not intrude upon an adult just because he is a child, nor may a child use pressure in the many ways in which a child can."

INTAIL is an acronym that means:
Ignore Now, Talk About It Later.

Listening Deep means listening without criticizing; without making judgments; without offering stock answers and clichés; without trying to convince someone of something; without trying to change the other person's feelings or ideas. When we listen deeply, we listen with our profoundest concentration; we listen with the depths of our whole being; we listen caringly. We hear the words and we feel the supercharged emotions underneath the words. And we respond to the child with our deepest sincerity, compassion, insight, and empathy.

Misbehavior is action that violates the principle of 'Freedom, not License', i.e., any action that hurts another person or living thing, or restricts the freedom of another person. What causes children's misbehavior? Erich Fromm writes: "Destructiveness is the outcome of unlived lives." A.S. Neill writes: "The difficult child is the child who is unhappy. He is at war with himself; and thus he is at war with the whole world." Of course, the caring grownup, knowing that unhappiness causes misbehavior, treats the root of the misbehavior by practicing the three essential goals of child maintenance: Prevent, Respond, Nourish.

Montagu's Maxim is a quote by Ashley Montagu:
"A human being should always respond, but never react."

Mother's Maxim is the most important idea for keeping children safe. Mother's Maxim says: "At all times, 24/7/366, know where your children are, and who they are with."

Natural consequences. A concept coined by Rudolf Dreikurs, natural consequences are the natural results of our behavior. For example, suppose in the evening I forget to buy milk — then the natural consequences of this carelessness is that in the morning there will be no milk for breakfast.

Needs of children. In addition to the basic need for an environment that allows the child to be safe and healthy, all children have six basic needs. 1) The need for love and friendship with grownups and other children. 2) The need to play. 3) The need for freedom to grow in their unique way. 4) The need to live and play in nature. 5) The need to cultivate their imagination and human feelings, by doing creative activities and the arts. 6) The need to learn how to think: how to make decisions, teach themselves, and solve problems.

OMY. An acronym that stands for "Ours, Mine, and Yours."
I tell the children that some of the group decisions will be Ours — decisions we make together, worked out to everyone's satisfaction. Some decisions will be all Mine (the child-maintenance worker's), and some decisions will be all Yours — decisions made by the child, or by a group of children together.

Opportunity-Problem (O-P) is any behavior problem or situation with an outcome that depends on the response of the grownup. React with force and punishment, and you worsen the behavior and antagonize the child. Respond with sincerity and kindness, and you help to heal the root of the misbehavior and deepen your rapport with the child.

Problematic Behavior (P-B) is a better term — more accurate and more comprehensive — for "misbehavior", because misbehavior implies that the problem is the fault of the child. Frequently, children have many problems that they did not cause. Problematic Behavior is any situation involving a child or children that requires care and attention from the grownups who care for them.

Resilience. What is resilience? Resilience is the inner strength — of body, heart, or mind — to bounce back and stand up again, after something hurts you and knocks you down. Whatever the problem is — a sudden sickness, a drastic change, or a storm of bad luck — resilient persons faces the challenges with honesty and courage. [Definition by MP]. Great CMWs always teach children the art of resilience.

Robot grownup. Any adult who reacts aggressively when kids misbehave, using the Way of Force.

Rumi's Reminder. Rumi has written: "Wherever you stand, be the soul of that place." The practical application of this wisdom, for all child-maintenance workers who care for kids, is this translation: "Pay attention, think ahead, and be the one in charge."

STM (Spontaneous Teachable Moment). An opportunity for child-maintenance workers to improvise an interesting lesson — to teach the child something about life, love, nature, or art.

Unconditional love. The robot grownup, if he cares at all, measures out his affection: he smiles to the child when the child does what he says, but he grows angry and unkind when the child misbehaves. The caring grownup accepts the child in all moments. To love a child unconditionally means that you are on the child's side no matter what the child says or does.

We Technique, the. A method for responding to misbehavior that lets the child or the children help the grownup to solve the problem. Do this by asking the child or children:

"We have a problem; what can we do to solve it?"

Zerp Factor. The Zerp Factor is the tendency of aggressive children — who desperately need caring human contact and affection — to not get that affection because their aggressive behavior drives children and adults away. (This comes from the character named Zerp in the novels *Lark's Magic,* and *Zen In The Art Of Child Maintenance.*) The antidotes to the Zerp Factor are to respond to the child with the three goals of Child Maintenance. (*See above*, Child maintenance, essential goals of).

Zerp's Law. Zerp's Law says: "When children misbehave they need more kindness, not less."

♥

Appendix A

101 Great Books For Children

1. The Adventures of Huckleberry Finn by Mark Twain
2. Adventures of Sherlock Holmes by A. Conan Doyle
3. Aesop's Fables by Aesop
4. Aladdin and The Wonderful Lamp
5. Alice's Adventures In Wonderland by Lewis Carroll
6. Andersen Fairy Tales by Hans Christian Andersen
7. Anne of Green Gables by Lucy Maud Montgomery
8. Arabian Nights Entertainments edited by Andrew Lang
9. At The Back Of The North Wind by George Macdonald
10. Autobiography of Benjamin Franklin by Benjamin Franklin
11. Beautiful Stories from Shakespeare by E. Nesbit
12. Beauty and The Beast by Mme. Le Prince de Beaumont
13. Black Beauty by Anna Sewell
14. The Blue Fairy Book by Andrew Lang.
15. The Bold Dragoon & Other Ghostly Tales by Washington Irving
16. The Borrowers by Mary Norton
17. Celtic Fairy Tales, & More Celtic Fairy Tales by Joseph Jacobs
18. Charlotte's Web by E. B. White
19. The Children's Homer by Padraic Colum
20. A Christmas Carol by Charles Dickens
21. The Crock Of Gold by James Stephens
22. The Cricket On The Hearth by Charles Dickens

23. Danish Fairy Tales by Svendt Grundtvig
24. David Copperfield by Charles Dickens
25. East O' The Sun, West O' The Moon by George Webbe Dasent
26. English Fairy Tales by Joseph Jacobs
27. Five Children and It by E. Nesbit
28. Five Little Peppers and How They Grew by Margaret Sidney
29. Golden Treasury Of Children's Literature by Louis Untermeyer
30. Great Expectations by Charles Dickens
31. Green Mansions by W. H. Hudson
32. Grimm's Fairy Tales by the Grimm Brothers
33. Hans Brinker by Mary M. Dodge
34. Haroun and the Sea of Stories by Salman Rushdie
35. Heidi by Johanna Spyri
36. The Hobbit by J. R. Tolkien
37. Indian Fairy Tales by Joseph Jacobs
38. Irish Fairy Tales by James Stephens
39. Jo's Boys by Louisa May Alcott
40. The Jungle Book by Rudyard Kipling
41. Just So Stories by Rudyard Kipling
42. Kidnapped by Robert Louis Stevenson
43. The King Of The Golden River by John Ruskin
44. King Solomon's Mines by H. Rider Haggard
45. Lark's Magic by Michael Pastore (Zorba Press)
46. The Light Princess by George MacDonald
47. Lincoln's Yarns and Stories by Alexander McClure
48. The Lion, The Witch, And The Wardrobe by C. S. Lewis
49. Little House on the Prairie by Laura Ingalls Wilder

50. The Little Prince by Antoine St. Exupery
51. Little Women by Louisa May Alcott
52. Lorna Doone by R. D. Blackmore
53. Lord Of The Rings by J. R. Tolkien
54. Luka and the Fire of Life by Salman Rushdie
55. The Maid of Sker by R. D. Blackmore
56. The Man Who Planted Trees by Jean Giono
57. Master of Ballantrae by Robert Louis Stevenson
58. The Merry Adventures Of Robin Hood by Howard Pyle
59. My Antonia by Willa Cather
60. Myths That Every Child Should Know by H. W. Mabie
61. Most Interesting Stories of All Nations by N. Hawthorne
62. The Nightingale by Hans Christian Andersen
63. The 1,001 Nights by Padraic Colum
64. Oliver Twist by Charles Dickens
65. The Odyssey by Homer, translated by W. H. D. Rouse
66. Old Hungarian Fairy Tales by Baroness Orczy
67. The Once And Future King by T. H. White
68. Perrault's Fairy Tales by Charles Perrault & G. Doré
69. Peter Pan by J. M. Barrie
70. The Adventures Of Pinocchio by Carlo Collodi
71. The Princess And The Curdie by George Macdonald
72. The Princess And The Goblin by George Macdonald
73. Ring Of Willows by Eric Barker
74. Robinson Crusoe by Daniel Defoe
75. The Rose and The Ring by W. M. Thackeray
76. The Secret Garden by Frances H. Burnett
77. The Selfish Giant by Oscar Wilde
78. She by H. Rider Haggard

79. The Snow Queen by Hans Christian Andersen
80. The Story Of A Bad Boy by Thomas Bailey Aldritch
81. Story Of My Life by Helen Keller
82. Story of The Champions of The Round Table by Howard Pyle
83. Story Of King Arthur And His Knights by Howard Pyle
84. Stuart Little by E. B. White
85. The Sword In The Stone by T. H. White
86. The Tales of Peter Rabbit by Beatrix Potter
87. The Three Musketeers by Alexandre Dumas père
88. Through The Looking Glass by Lewis Carroll
89. Tom Brown's School Days by Thomas Hughes
90. Treasure Island by Robert Louis Stevenson
91. The Trumpet Of The Swan by E. B. White
92. The Twenty-One Balloons by William Pene du Bois
93. Twenty Thousand Leagues Under The Sea by Jules Verne
94. Uncle Remus, His Songs And Sayings by Joel Chandler Harris
95. Uncle Tom's Cabin by Harriet Beecher Stowe
96. The Water Babies by Charles Kingsley
97. Watership Down by Richard Adams
98. The Wind In The Willows by Kenneth Grahame
99. A Wonder Book by Nathaniel Hawthorne
100. The Wonderful Wizard Of Oz by Frank L. Baum
101. World Tales by Idries Shah
102. Zlateh The Goat And Other Stories by Isaac B. Singer

Appendix B

101 Great Films for Children

1. Adventures of Robin Hood (1938)
2. Akeelah and the Bee (2006)
3. Aladdin (1992)
4. Alice in Wonderland (1951)
5. Anne of Green Gables (1934)
6. Back to the Future 1 (1985)
7. Back to the Future 2
8. Back to the Future 3
9. Bambi (1942)
10. Beauty and the Beast (1991)
11. Beauty and the Beast (2017)
12. Breadwinner, The (2017) PG-13
13. Bringing up Baby (1938)
14. Captains Courageous (1937)
15. Charlotte's Web (1973)
16. Children of Heaven (1997)
17. Christmas Carol, A (1951)
18. Color of Paradise, The (1999)
19. Darby O'Gill and the Little People (1959)
20. David Copperfield (1935)
21. Despicable Me (2010)
22. E.T. the Extra-terrestrial (1982)
23. Fantasia (1940)
24. Fiddler on the Roof
25. Finding Dory (2016)
26. Finding Nemo (2003)
27. Flora & Ulysses (2021)
28. Frozen (2013)
29. General, The (1926)

30. Goonies, The (1985)
31. Great Expectations (1946)
32. Greatest Showman, The (2017)
33. He Named Me Malala
34. How Green Was My Valley (1941)
35. Howl's Moving Castle (2004, dir. Hayao Miyazaki)
36. Hugo (2011)
37. Humpbacked Horse, The (1975)
38. Indiana Jones and the Raiders of the Lost Ark (1981)
39. Inside Out (2015)
40. Iron Giant, The (1999)
41. It's A Wonderful Life (1946, Capra)
42. James and the Giant Peach (1996)
43. Jumanji (1995)
44. Jungle Book, The (1967)
45. Karate Kid, The (1984)
46. Kes (1969)
47. Kid, The (1921)
48. Kirikou and the Sorceress (1998)
49. Lady and the Tramp (1955)
50. Lego Movie, The (2014)
51. Life, Animated (2016)
52. Lion King, The (1994)
53. Little Mermaid, The (1989)
54. Little Prince, The (2015)
55. Little Princess, A (1995)
56. Little Women (1994)
57. Lost Horizon
58. Man Who Planted Trees, The
59. March of the Penguins
60. Mary Poppins
61. Microcosmos (1996)
62. Moana (2016)
63. Muppet Christmas Carol, The (1992)
64. Muppet Movie, The (1979)

65. My Fair Lady (1964)
66. My Life as a Zucchini (2016)
67. My Life as a Dog (1985)
68. My Neighbour Totoro (1988)
69. National Velvet (1944)
70. Nausicaa and the Valley of the Wind (1984, by Hayao Miyazaki)
71. Oliver! (1968)
72. Oliver Twist (1948)
73. One Hundred and One Dalmatians (1961)
74. Paddington (2014)
75. Pather Panchali (India)
76. Peter Pan (1953)
77. Pinocchio (1940)
78. Princess Bride, The (1987)
79. Princess Mononoke (1997 by Hayao Miyazaki)
80. Railway Children, The (1970)
81. Ratatouille (2007)
82. Rodgers & Hammerstein's Cinderella (2004)
83. Red Balloon, The (1956)
84. Red Balloon, The (2006)
85. Robin Hood (1973)
86. Secret Garden, The (1993)
87. Secret Life of Bees, The (2008) PG-13
88. Secret of NIMH, The (1982)
89. Secret World of Arrietty, The (2010)
90. Singin' in the Rain
91. Snow White and the Seven Dwarfs (1937)
92. Soul (2020)
93. Song of Sparrows, The (2008) Iran
94. Sound of Music, The (1965)
95. Sounder (1972)
96. Spirit of the Beehive, The (1973)
97. Spirited Away (2001, by Hayao Miyazaki)
98. Star Trek II: The Wrath of Khan (1982)

99. Superman (1978)
100. Swiss Family Robinson (1960)
101. Sword in the Stone, The (1963)
102. Tangled (2010)
103. Thief of Bagdad, The (1940)
104. To Kill a Mockingbird (1962)
105. Toy Story (1995)
106. Toy Story 2 (1999)
107. Toy Story 3
108. Toy Story 4
109. Treasure Island (1934)
110. Up (2008)
111. Wadjda (2012)
112. WALL·E (2008)
113. Wallace & Gromit: The Curse of the Were-Rabbit (2005)
114. Watership Down (1978)
115. Where Is the Friend's House? (1987)
116. Whisper of the Heart (1995 by Hayao Miyazaki)
117. White Balloon, The (1995, Iran)
118. Willy Wonka & the Chocolate Factory (1971)
119. Wind in the Willows (1988)
120. Wind Rises, The (2013 by Hayao Miyazaki)
121. Wizard of Oz, The (1939, dir. Victor Fleming)
122. Wonder (2017)
123. Your Name (2016)
124. Zarafa (2012)

♥

Appendix C

101 Great Books for Adults

1. Andersen, Hans Christian — Fairy Tales
2. Anonymous — 1001 Nights of Adventure (Arabian Nights)
3. Aristophanes — Lysistrata
4. Arnold, Matthew — Culture and Anarchy
5. Austen, Jane — Emma
6. Balzac, Honore de — Father Goriot
7. Blake, William — Poems
8. Boccaccio, Giovanni — The Decameron
9. Bronte, Charlotte — Jayne Eyre
10. Bronte, Emily — Wuthering Heights
11. Buber, Martin — I and Thou
12. Cary, Joyce — The Horse's Mouth
13. Casanova — Memoirs (translated by Willard Trask)
14. Cervantes, Miguel de — Don Quixote
15. Charriere, Henri — Papillon
16. Dante — The Divine Comedy
17. Dickens, Charles — Great Expectations
18. Dostoyevsky, Feodor — The Brothers Karamazov
19. Durant, Will — The Story of Philosophy
20. Eliot, George — Middlemarch
21. Emerson, Ralph Waldo — Essays
22. Euripides — The Bacchae
23. Fielding, Henry — Tom Jones
24. Flaubert, Gustave — Madame Bovary
25. Forster, E. M. — Howard's End

26. Frank, Anne — The Diary of a Young Girl
27. Franklin, Benjamin — Autobiography
28. Fromm, Erich — The Art Of Loving
29. Gandhi — Autobiography
30. Giono, Jean — The Song of the World
31. Goethe, J. W. von — Faust
32. Goethe, J. W. von — Wilhelm Meister's Apprenticeship
33. Goldsmith, Oliver — The Vicar of Wakefield
34. Gontcharoff, Ivan — A Common Story
35. Gorky, Maxim — Autobiography
36. Haggard, Rider — She
37. Hamsun, Knut — Growth of the Soil
38. Hawthorne, Nathaniel — The Scarlet Letter
39. Herodotus — The Persian Wars
40. Hesse, Hermann — Narcissus and Goldmund
41. Homer — The Odyssey
42. Hudson, William Henry — Green Mansions
43. Huxley, Aldous — Brave New World
44. Ibsen, Henrik — Hedda Gabler
45. Jacobsen, Jens Peter — Niels Lyhne
46. Joyce, James — Ulysses
47. Kazantzakis, Nikos — The Odyssey, A Modern Sequel
48. Kazantzakis, Nikos — Zorba the Greek
49. Keats, John — Poems
50. Keller, Helen — The Story of My Life
51. Lao Tzu — Tao Te Ching
52. Lawrence, D.H. — Women In Love
53. London, Jack — Martin Eden
54. Mann, Thomas — The Magic Mountain
55. Manzoni, Alessandro — The Betrothed
56. Marx, Karl — Das Kapital

57. Maskaleris, Thanasis — The Terrestrial Gospel of Nikos Kazantzakis
58. Melville, Herman — Moby Dick
59. Miller, Henry — The Colossus of Maroussi
60. Montagu, Ashley — Growing Young
61. More, Thomas — Utopia
62. Morris, William — News From Nowhere
63. Neill, A.S. — Summerhill
64. Nietzsche, Friedrich — Thus Spake Zarathustra
65. Oppenheim, E. Phillips — The Great Impersonation
66. Pastore, Michael — Zen in the Art of Child Maintenance
67. Pastore, Michael — Thoreau Bound: A Utopian Romance in the Isles of Greece
68. Plato — The Dialogues
69. Plutarch — Lives of the Noble Greeks and Romans
70. Powys, John Cowper — Wolf Solent
71. Proust, Marcel — In Search of Lost Time
72. Pushkin, Alexander Sergeyevich — Eugene Onegin
73. Pyle, Howard — Robin Hood
74. Rabelais — Gargantua and Pantagruel
75. Read, Herbert — The Green Child
76. Rolland, Romain — Jean Christophe
77. Rostand, Edmund — Cyrano de Bergerac
78. Rousseau, Jean Jaques — Emile
79. Rushdie, Salman — The Enchantress of Florence
80. Ruskin, John — Unto This Last
81. Russell, Bertrand — Autobiography
82. Sand, George — Consuelo
83. Sand, Geogre — The Countess of Rudolstadt
84. Scott, Walter — Ivanhoe
85. Shakespeare, William — (all his plays and poems)
86. Shaw, Bernard — Man and Superman

87. Shaw, Bernard — Saint Joan
88. Shelley, Mary — Frankenstein; or, The Modern Prometheus
89. Shelley, Percy Bysshe — Poems
90. Silone, Ignazio — Bread and Wine
91. Smith, Huston — The World's Religions
92. Steinbeck, John — The Grapes of Wrath
93. Stendhal (Marie Henri Beyle) — The Charterhouse of Parma
94. Sterne, Lawrence — Tristam Shandy
95. Thoreau, Henry David — Walden
96. Tobias, Michael Charles — Adventures of Mr Marigold
97. Tobias, Michael Charles — The Earth in Fragments : A
    Memoir by Michael Charles Tobias
98. Tolstoy, Leo — War and Peace
99. Turgenev, Ivan — Fathers and Sons
100.Twain, Mark (Samuel Clemens) — Adventures of
    Huckleberry Finn
101.Uris, Leon — Exodus
102.Van Gogh, Vincent — Letters
103. Voltaire — Candide
104. Ward, Lynd — (all his graphic novels)
105. Wells, H.G. — Ann Veronica : A Modern Love Story
106. West, Nathaniel — Miss Lonelyhearts
107. Whitman, Walt — Leaves of Grass
108. Wilde, Oscar — The Importance of Being Earnest
109. Wolfe, Thomas — Look Homeward Angel
110. Woolf, Virginia — To The Lighthouse
111. Wordsworth, William — The Prelude
112. Yeats, William Butler — Poems
113. Yezierska, Anzia — Bread Givers
114. Yutang, Lin — The Importance of Living
115. Zweig, Stefan — Master Builders

Appendix D

101 Great Films for Adults

An * tells that the movie is all comedy or a partial comedy.

1. Adventures of Robin Hood (1938) *
2. All About Eve (1950)
3. Amelie (2001) *
4. Anari (1959) *
5. Andrei Rublev (1966, Tarkovsky)
6. As Good As It Gets
7. Back to the Future 1 (1985) *
8. Battleship Potemkin (1925)
9. Ben-Hur (1959)
10. Black
11. Black Narcissus
12. Blade Runner (1982)
13. Brave New World (1980) *
14. Bread and Chocolate *
15. Brothers Karamazov, The
16. Burnt by the Sun
17. Casablanca (1942, dir. Michael Curtiz)
18. Christmas Carol, A (1951) *
19. Cinema Paradiso (1988, dir. Giuseppe Tornatore)
20. Citizen Kane (1941, dir. Orson Welles)
21. City Lights (Chaplin) *

22. City of Lost Children (1995, dirs. Marc Caro, Jean-Pierre Jeunet) *
23. Crouching Tiger, Hidden Dragon (China, 2001)
24. Cyrano de Bergerac (1950, dir. Michael Gordon) *
25. Day at the Races, A (1947, Marx Brothers) *
26. Dead Poets Society (1989, dir. Peter Weir)
27. Doctor Zhivago (1965, dir. David Lean)
28. Duck Soup (1933, Marx Brothers) *
29. English Patient, The
30. Eternal Sunshine of the Spotless Mind *
31. Exodus
32. Fanny and Alexander (1982, Bergman)
33. Fences (2016)
34. Fiddler on the Roof *
35. 400 Blows, The (Truffaut)
36. Fugitive, The (1993)
37. Gandhi
38. Gattaca (1997)
39. General, The (1926) *
40. Gold Rush (Chaplin) *
41. Goldfinger (1964)
42. Gone With The Wind (1939, dir. Victor Fleming)
43. Grapes of Wrath, The
44. Great Dictator, The (Chaplin) *
45. Greatest Show on Earth, The
46. Harold and Maude (1971, dir. Hal Ashby) *
47. Harrison Bergeron *
48. Her (2013)
49. His Girl Friday (1940) *

50. How Green Was My Valley (1941)
51. Illusionist, The (2006, dir. Neil Burger) *
52. Immortal Beloved (1994, dir. Bernard Rose)
53. Importance of Being Earnest, The *
54. Indian Epic (by Fritz Lang. This is the 1959 edition, that runs for 201 minutes.)
55. It's A Wonderful Life (Capra) *
56. Jean de Florette (1986)
57. Jules and Jim (Truffaut) *
58. Kaos (1984)
59. Kid, The (Chaplin) *
60. King of Hearts (1966, dir. Philippe de Broca) *
61. Kiss Me Kate (1953) *
62. Lady Eve, The (1941, dir. Preston Sturges) *
63. Life Is Beautiful *
64. Little Big Man (1970) *
65. Little Women (three excellent films in 1949, 1994, 2019)
66. Limelight (1952, dir. Charlie Chaplin) *
67. Long Day's Journey Into Night (2014)
68. Lost Horizon (1937) *
69. Man For All Seasons, A (1966, dir. Fred Zinnemann)
70. Manon of the Spring (1986)
71. Mary Poppins *
72. Matrix, The (1999)
73. Metropolis (1927, dir. Fritz Lang)
74. Midnight in Paris (2011) *
75. Midnight's Children (2012, dir. Deepa Mehta)
76. Modern Times (1936, dir. Charlie Chaplin) *
77. My Dinner With Andre *

78. My Fair Lady (1964) *
79. My Man Godfrey (1936, dir. Gregory La Cava)*
80. Network (1976, dir. Sidney Lumet)
81. Night at the Opera, A (1935, Marx Brothers) *
82. On The Waterfront (1954, dir. Elia Kazan)
83. Our Mutual Friend (1998, novel by Charles Dickens, dir. Julian Farino)
84. Pan's Labyrinth
85. Pather Panchali (1954)
86. Persepolis (2007)
87. Philadelphia Story, The (1940)
88. Picture of Dorian Gray, The (1945, dir. Albert Lewin) *
89. Plague Dogs, The (1982)
90. Postman, The/IL Postino (1994, dir. Michael Radford) *
91. Pygmalion (1938, dir. Anthony Asquith, Leslie Howard) *
92. Rab ni Bana di Jodi
93. Rashomon (1950)
94. RockStar
95. Roman Holiday *
96. Saving Private Ryan (1998)
97. Scent of A Woman
98. Schindler's List (1993)
99. Seventh Seal, The (1957, Bergman)
100. Shawshank Redemption, The (1994)
101. Siddhartha (1972, dir. Conrad Rooks)
102. Slumdog Millionaire
103. Smiles of A Summer Night (Bergman) *
104. Sound of Music, The *
105. Soylent Green

106. Spirited Away (2001, Miyazaki)

107. Starmaker

108. Spartacus (1960, dir. Stanley Kubrick)

109. Spellbound (1945, dir. Alfred Hitchcock)

110. Star Trek II: The Wrath of Khan (1982)

111. Sting, The (1973, dir. George Roy Hill) *

112. Suddenly, Last Summer (1960)

113. Sullivan's Travels (1941, dir. Preston Sturges) *

114. Taare Zameen Par

115. Ten Commandments, The (1956)

116. Things to Come

117. Time After Time (1979, dir. Nicholas Meyer) *

118. Tiger in the Snow *

119. To Be or Not to Be (dir. Lubitsch) *

120. To Kill A Mockingbird (1962)

121. To Live

122. Tokyo Story (1953)

123. Tree Grows in Brooklyn, A (1945)

124. Watership Down (1978)

125. West Side Story (1961, dirs. Jerome Robbins, Robert Wise)

126. Wings of Desire (1987, dir. Wim Wenders)

127. Wizard of Oz, The (1939, dir. Victor Fleming) *

128. Women in Love

129. You Can't Take It With You *

130. Zorba the Greek (1964, dir. Michael Cacoyannis) *

Bibliography of Interesting Books about Children and Childhood

1. Aries, Philip. Centuries of Childhood (1962).
2. Bettelheim, Bruno. The Uses of Enchantment.
3. Bronfenbrenner, Urie. Two Worlds of Childhood (1972).
4. Buscaglia, Leo. Living, Loving, and Learning.
5. Coles, Robert. The Moral Intelligence of Children.
6. Dickens, Charles. David Copperfield.
7. Dreikurs, Rudolf R. & Vicki Soltz. Children the Challenge.
8. Erikson, Erik H. Childhood and Society (2nd edition).
9. Fromm, Erich. The Art Of Loving.
10. Fynn. Mister God, This is Anna.
11. Ginott, Haim G. Between Parent and Child.
12. Goodman, Paul. Growing Up Absurd.
13. Greven, Philip. Spare The Child (1990).
14. Hazard, Paul. Books, Children, and Men.
15. Healy, Jane M. Endangered Minds.
16. Hesse, Hermann. Siddhartha: An Indian Tale.
17. Huizinga, Johan. Homo Ludens: A Study of the Play Element of Culture.
18. Huxley, Aldous. Young Archimedes (short story).
19. Hyman, Irwin A. The Case Against Spanking.
20. James, Muriel and Dorothy Jongeward. Born To Win: Transactional Analysis With Gestalt Experiments.
21. Jung, Carl Gustav. The Development of Personality.
22. Kohl, Herbert and Colin Greer. The Plain Truth of Things.
23. Kohn, Alfie. Beyond Discipline.
24. Konner, Melvin. The Evolution of Childhood.
25. Lane, Homer. Talks to Parents and Teachers.
26. Lasch, Christopher. Haven In A Heartless World.

27. LeShan, Eda J. The Conspiracy Against Childhood.

28. LeShan, Eda J. When Your Child Drives You Crazy.

29. Louv, Richard. Last Child in the Woods: Saving Our Children from Nature-Deficit Disorder.

30. Maté, Gabor. Scattered : How Attention Deficit Disorder Originates And What You Can Do About It

31. Mearns, Hughes. Creative Power (2nd revised edition).

32. Menninger, Karl. Man Against Himself.

33. Millar, Susanna. The Psychology of Play.

34. Miller, Alice. For Your Own Good.

35. Miller, Alice. Thou Shalt Not Be Aware: Society's Betrayal of the Child.

36. Miller, Alice. The Truth Will Set You Free: Overcoming Emotional Blindness and Finding Your True Adult Self.

37. Miller, Alice. The Untouched Key: Tracing Childhood Trauma in Creativity and Destructiveness.

38. Montagu, Ashley. Growing Young (2nd Edition).

39. Montessori, Maria. The Secret of Childhood.

40. Neill, A.S. Neill, Neill, Orange Peel! (Neill's autobiography).

41. Neill, A.S. Summerhill: A Radical Approach to Child Rearing (with a Foreword by Erich Fromm).

42. Noddings, Nel. Happiness and Education.

43. Paideia: The Ideals of Greek Culture (3 volumes).

44. Pastore, Michael. 101 Answers in Child Maintenance.

45. Pastore, Michael. 101 Problems in Child Maintenance.

46. Pastore, Michael. Child Maintenance : How to Respond to Misbehavior without Using Force, Rewards, or Punishments.

47. Pastore, Michael. Instant Drama.

48. Pastore, Michael. Kids Play Games.

49. Pastore, Michael. Lark's Magic (novel for children).

50. Pastore, Michael. Teaching Kindness and Peace.

51. Pastore, Michael. Zen In The Art of Child Maintenance (novel for adults).
52. Pearce, Joseph Chilton. Evolution's End.
53. Pearce, Joseph Chilton. Magical Child.
54. Piaget, Jean. The Psychology of the Child.
55. Postman, Neil. Building a Bridge to the Eighteenth Century
56. Postman, Neil. The Disappearance Of Childhood.
57. Postman, Neil. Technopoly : the Surrender of Culture to Technology.
58. Read, Herbert. Education Through Art.
59. Redl, Fritz and David Wineman. Controls From Within: Techniques for the Treatment of the Aggressive Child.
60. Reik, Theodor. Listening With the Third Ear.
61. Riak, Jordan. Plain Talk about Spanking (2011 edition).
62. Rousseau, Jean-Jaques. Emile.
63. Russell, Bertrand. Education (1916).
64. Seligman, Martin E. P. The Optimistic Child: A Proven Program to Safeguard Children Against Depression and Build Lifelong Resilience.
65. Sharenow, Arthur. 37 Summers: My Years as a Camp Director.
66. Shaw, George Bernard. Parents and Children.
67. Sommerville, C. John. The Rise and Fall of Childhood
68. Straus, Murray. Beating The Devil Out Of Them (2000)
69. Truffaut, Francois. The 400 Blows (book of the screenplay).
70. UNICEF. State of the World's Children 2017 : Children in a Digital World. A free download from https://www.unicef.org/sowc2017/
71. Winnicott, D.W. Talking to Parents.
72. Winnicott, D.W. Thinking About Children.
73. Zax, Melvin. The Psychology of Discipline.

QNI (Questions, Notes, Ideas)

QNI (Questions, Notes, Ideas)

Index

B

Baldwin, James, 160
Balzac, Honoré de, 126
Beccaria, Cesare, 158
Benigni, Roberto, 122
Bettelheim, Bruno, 135, 170
bibliophiles, trigger warning for, 146
Bismarck, Otto von, 155
Blake, William, 140, 155
Bloom, Harold, 148
Bond, James, 5
books for adults, 101 great, 193
books for children, 101 great, 185
Brave New World (Huxley), 175
bribery, 65
Broken Racket, A (Opportunity-Problem # 7), 75, 108, 115
Buber, Martin, 86

C

C.A.R.I.N.G. 6-Step Strategy, 24
caring grownup, 13, 178, 183
caring response, 178
Carlsen, Magnus, 117
Carson, Rachel, 155
Casals, Pablo, 122, 162
change the circumstances, 12 questions, 39
Change the Circumstances, Technique of, 26, 27, 35, 37, 38, 39, 40, 104
Chesterton, G. K., 42
child abuse, 111, 121, 131
child maintenance, defined, 9–10, 12, 179
child maintenance, essential goals of, 12, 179
child-maintenance worker (CMW), defined, 12, 179
Childhood (Tolstoy), 158
CMW, defined, 12, 179

♥

Zorba Press Books
about Children and Childhood

Lark's Magic
ZP-001 (novel for children)

Zen in the Art of Child Maintenance
ZP-002 (novel for adults)

Kids Play Games :
101 Active Games for Happy Children
ZP-003 ... 2nd edition (2021)

Child Maintenance :
How to Respond to Misbehavior Without Force,
Rewards, or Punishments
ZP-004

101 Problems in Child Maintenance :
Real-Life Training Situations for Everyone Who Works
With Kids
ZP-005

101 Answers in Child Maintenance :
Answer Guide to 101 Problems in Child Maintenance
ZP-006

Instant Drama :
a Funny Book of Drama Games and Writing Games for
Creative Kids
ZP-007

Teaching Kindness and Peace :
How Stories Cultivate Creativity and Prevent Violence
ZP-008

Camp Counselor Smart Guide :
How to Work and Play With Kids at Summer Camps
ZP-009

Kids Write Poems
ZP-010

Also Published by Zorba Press

Zenlightenment :
Mind-Opening Insights about Life, Love & Happiness

The Zorba Anthology of Love Stories

The Ithaca Manual of Style :
Writing Fiction and Nonfiction that is Clear, Concise,
and Captivating

https://ZorbaPress.com

www.ingramcontent.com/pod-product-compliance
Lightning Source LLC
Chambersburg PA
CBHW020154090426
42734CB00008B/816